THE SEVEN DEADLY SINS

THE SEVEN DEADLY SINS
a visitor's guide

LAWRENCE S. CUNNINGHAM

ave maria press AmP notre dame, indiana

Founded in 1865, Ave Maria Press is a ministry of the United States Province of Holy Cross.

www.avemariapress.com

Paperback: ISBN-10 1-59471-340-5, ISBN-13 978-1-59471-1-340-8

E-book: ISBN-10 1-59471-359-6, ISBN-13 978-1-59471-359-0

Cover image © Veer

Cover and text design by Brian C. Conley.

Printed and bound in the United States of America.

Library of Congress Cataloging-in-Publication Data
Cunningham, Lawrence.
    The seven deadly sins : a visitor's guide / Lawrence S. Cunningham.
        p. cm.
    Includes bibliographical references.
    ISBN 978-1-59471-340-8 (pbk.) -- ISBN 1-59471-340-5 (pbk.)
    1. Deadly sins. 2. Catholic Church--Doctrines. I. Title.
    BV4626.C86 2012
    241'.3--dc23

                                    2012022140

CONTENTS

ACKNOWLEDGMENTS

One sure remedy for sin is gratitude, and in the making of this little book there is no end to the list of others who require thanks. First, I am grateful that *Notre Dame Business* permitted me to use material once published in their magazine. Second, the editors at Ave Maria Press, and Patrick McGowan in particular, encouraged me to work on this material, and then they saw it through to finish in such a professional fashion. Of course, I am deeply indebted to the Department of Theology at the University of Notre Dame for having given me such a welcoming home—within which I worked until my retirement in 2011. Finally, I am inordinately proud of Cecilia, my wife and helpmate, and our girls, Sarah and Julia, whose love has kept this pride from being a sin.

INTRODUCTION

David Fincher's 1995 film, *Seven*, chronicles a serial killer who chooses victims that exemplify each of the seven deadly sins. To narrate a terrible story set in contemporary times, Fincher examines a hallowed tradition of a moral category whose history dates back to the late fourth century. An earlier retelling is the 1933 ballet *The Seven Deadly Sins*, choreographed by George Balanchine, with music composed by Kurt Weill and words by Bertolt Brecht. It's the story of two sisters who committed the seven sins in different cities. The ballet's creative team and the filmmaker drew upon commonplace beliefs in the medieval world. Dante used the seven deadly sins to organize his *Purgatorio*, the second part of the *Divine Comedy*. In *The Canterbury Tales*, Chaucer has the good Parson preach an edifying sermon on the sins. In Bunyan's *The Pilgrim's Progress*, we meet the sins personified. The sinful list has lingered into our own time and, as we shall see, shows up in various ways.

It was of significant interest to medieval thinkers that the sins numbered to seven. With a keen interest in St. Augustine's exploration into the mystical meaning of numbers, medieval commentators were able to contrast the seven deadly sins with the seven penitential psalms, the seven petitions of the Lord's Prayer, or, more typically, the seven gifts of the Holy Spirit (Is 11:2–3) or the seven corporal works of mercy (and, later, the seven spiritual works of mercy) or the seven last words of Jesus upon the Cross. That the naming of the sins and their counterparts did not comport easily was of little concern—it was the potency of the number seven that counted, since the Bible opens with the six days of creation and the added day of Sabbath rest.

Of more interest, however, is to explain the origins of these seven death-dealing sins named traditionally as pride, envy, wrath, sloth, avarice, gluttony, and lust. The list as such has no *single* biblical warrant, although each is mentioned as a sin in various books of the Bible. The origins of the list are to be found in the work of that great monastic writer and saint of late antiquity, John Cassian (ca. 360–435), who, with long experience in the Christian East among the Desert Fathers, in 415 wrote the *Institutes*, a treatise on the monastic life, after he had settled in Marseille—where he had founded two monasteries.

Borrowing heavily from the writings of the Greek monk Evagrius of Pontus (345–399), John Cassian said that the goal of the monastic life was to attain "purity of heart" because Jesus had said that those who attained purity of heart would "see God" (Mt 5:8). However, there were obstacles to attaining purity of heart caused by phantasms or passions (Evagrius called them, in Greek, *logismoi*) that clouded the heart. Evagrius and John Cassian both describe these *logismoi* as eight in number: gluttony, fornication, avarice, anger, dejection (sadness), *acedia* (boredom), vainglory, and pride.

A later, seventh-century monastic writer named John Climacus described these obstructions and how they functioned by explaining how a certain suggestion comes to the mind (e.g., let me seek out some unlawful pleasure) while the mind plays with the desirability of the pleasure. The mind then consents to the suggestion, and after an interior struggle (I should not do this, but maybe . . .), finally, one is captivated by the temptation or, in the words of John Climacus in *The Ladder of Divine Ascent*, the suggestion captivates the heart.

For these monastic writers, the eight *logismoi* were not exactly understood as *sins*, but as powerful imaginative constructs or passions that clouded the mind (they would say "the heart") and led to misguided plans of action. If acted upon, they did lead to sin. Those writers saw the eight *logismoi* as veils, illusions, and passions that clouded the heart and, as such, blocked that purity of heart by which one came to an experiential knowledge of God dwelling in the heart. To read the *Institutes* is to read a treatise that reflects a powerful psychological insight into wayward interior motives. In time, these subtle explorations into illusions would become known as "deadly sins," but in their origin they were considered more of a prelude to sin.

John Cassian's works had a powerful influence on later monasticism. The *Rule of St. Benedict*—the foundational guide for subsequent monastic life in the West—pays tribute to Cassian. It was Pope Gregory the Great (ca. 540–604), himself once a monk and biographer of St. Benedict, who changed the list of the eight *logismoi* into the seven sins we know today. In a vast, sprawling work glossing over the Book of Job—known as the *Moralia in Job*—Gregory collapsed vainglory and pride into pride alone and folded dejection (sadness) into *acedia* while adding the sin of envy, thus making the list as we know it today. Gregory also argued that the root of all these sins was pride. Such was the authority of Gregory and his *Moralia* that the list of seven sins became standard in the West. He saw these sins as "capital" (from the Latin *caput*—head), as the source of all other sins. St. Thomas Aquinas would repeat Gregory's observation that from these sins all sorts of other sins would come.

CASSIAN TO GREGORY: EIGHT *LOGISMOI* TO SEVEN SINS

JOHN CASSIAN

Gluttony
Lust
Avarice
Wrath
Sadness
Sloth
Vainglory
Pride

GREGORY THE GREAT

Vainglory (pride)
Envy
Sadness (sloth)
Avarice
Wrath
Lust
Gluttony

Of course, there is nothing sacrosanct or doctrinally binding about the list. Indeed, the late political theorist and philosopher Judith Shklar, in her collected essays *Ordinary Vices*, singled out cruelty, hypocrisy, snobbery, betrayal, and misanthropy as particularly noxious—both for individuals and society. It takes only a moment's reflection, however, to understand that something as powerful as hatred can flow from envy or wrath, just as egomania is but a contemporary way of describing pride or greed. Those permutations are numerous, and our only reason for writing these chapters on the traditional seven is to give us latitude to observe behavior in our contemporary setting. In other words, the list of seven sins is not normative but suggestive.

Whether following the traditional litany of sins or not, contemporary writers, both theologians and ethicists, have exhibited a continuing interest in ruminating on virtues and vices. *Deadly Vices*, a recent book by the British philosopher Gabriele Taylor, states that the seven deadly sins are still worthy of consideration because, as Taylor writes in her introduction, "these so-called deadly sins were correctly so named and correctly classed together. Irrespective of their theological background they can be seen to be similar in structure in their agent's thoughts and desires while differing in content depending on the vice in question, with focus primarily on the self and its position in the world. They are similar also in that in each case, they are destructive of that self and prevent its flourishing."[1] The key idea in Taylor's statement is that these sins retard or destroy the flourishing of the self. In a nutshell: succumbing to these passions is not wholesome. They shrivel us as humans.

The following essays on the seven deadly sins originally appeared in a much-abbreviated form in the magazine *Notre Dame Business*. Carolyn Woo, then dean of the Mendoza College of Business, thought that the magazine ought to have a theological voice and invited me to write for it. When the series was complete, the editors of Ave Maria Press thought it might be useful to expand the series into a brief book for more general circulation. I was happy to comply with that request. My intention is not to add new insights into a vast collection of literature on the seven deadly sins, but to think about them in a pastorally sensitive fashion. To do that means that we must consider both the sins themselves and their mirror opposites: the virtues that correspond positively to them. Two more sections have been added as the essays have been expanded. A chapter to conclude the book has been included on that primordial virtue of "purity of heart," lest the seven sins have the last word. After that chapter, a bibliographical excursion has been offered to give the reader a small glance into the vast scholarship and commentary on the seven deadly sins.

The editors made the brilliant suggestion that the subtitle be "A Visitor's Guide" to honor Dante—who did visit the territory of purgatory where these sins were expiated. Dante climbed the seven terraces of the mount and at each terrace encountered each of the sins and examples of their virtuous remedy. I would only add that, since we are all visitors on this earth, we too will eventually meet the seven sins—either directly or in their many disguises.

An inside joke within our department: a colleague would inquire, "What are you working on?" My reply would be: "Lust." At a more serious level, however, it was a pleasure to rummage around in the history of the theological tradition that is rooted in monastic theology, to muse over the ways, literary and visual, that the seven deadly sins became treated, and to have the chance to enter, albeit with great caution, into the area of Christian ethics—while, at the same time, being aware that a daily inspection of the news or even a daily examination of conscience reminded me that the human capacity for sin seems unabated. With this caution in mind, I must point out to the reader that I am neither an ethicist nor a moral theologian by profession or training. My interest in this topic arose out of interest in the history of Christian spirituality in general and monastic spirituality in particular. I have no particular expertise in the area of Christian ethics. Indeed, I have been stung by a comment once made by Meister Eckhart when he commented on the Pauline demand to put on the armor of God. Eckhart said that too many have the armor closed in a closet or on a stand for display. He then added: "There are those who have virtues in their notebooks or who only know and talk about them." With that admonitory thought in mind, I write on the virtues needed to cultivate as one confronts the deadly sins.

ONE

SOME GRATIFYING THOUGHTS ON GLUTTONY

Their end is destruction; their god is their stomach.

PHILIPPIANS 3:19

Although I confess to a mild predilection for watching sports on television, certain events cause me to reach immediately for the remote because of their sheer capacity to bore. I would rather look at old magazines in a dentist's office than watch—this is a selective list—poker, bowling, or golf on television. In my random cruising around the channels, however, a new phenomenon has caught my eye that is beyond boring; it is disgusting: competitive eating. Whatever possesses people to try to eat dozens of hot dogs in a limited period of time? Is there not something revolting about such an enterprise?

To my queasy horror, not only have hot-dog-eating contests become popular on television, but also they have actually been deemed sporting contests. To add insult to injury, there was a series on the Travel Channel featuring a rather porcine young man who accepted challenges in various eateries around the country to finish impossible confections of food in a set period of time. It is evidently thought that a human being sitting down in front of a six-pound sandwich with appropriate sides—and stuffing the mixture in his face in an hour—is a feat to be admired.

I often wonder who it is who wishes to watch these folks shovel food in their faces, not for nutrition or pleasure, or the joy of eating in company, but simply to ingest large quantities of "food." If there is any sign of the coming apocalypse, in my estimation, eating contests rank high on the list. Such contests constitute a travesty against the very nature of eating; they dramatically demonstrate the classic definition of gluttony: the *inordinate* appetite for food. Such feats are neither for nutrition nor for hospitality, but for the sheer purpose of stuffing food into the body. Furthermore, such feats abuse the very notion of food in itself and, in the process, abase food. When moms told their children not to waste food ("Think of the starving children . . ."), as moms often did, they articulated a profound truth.

To my mind, one of the greatest human pleasures is to eat good food, and especially if that eating is done in the company of people. After all, the word "companion" means "one with whom we share bread." That kind of eating, as the traditional Catholic blessing rightly says, is a "gift" that comes from God's "bounty." More than half-a-dozen times in Luke's gospel, Jesus enjoys the hospitality of others. He shares bread with both sinners and Pharisees. Luke's marvelous account of the Emmaus encounter (Lk 24:13–33) insists that the companions of Jesus "recognized him in the breaking of bread." The British theologian Nicholas Lash once remarked of that meeting on the road to Emmaus that the Church was born in an act of hospitality. Jesus Christ is a companion (from the Latin *cum pane*—a bread sharer) and a brother (from the old Germanic root *brōt*—bread). And, not to put too fine a point on it, he gives us himself as bread: "Take and eat. . . ." Eating, in that sense of the term, is fundamental to a full human life.

One could make the argument that the sheer joy of eating a festive meal—think of Christmas dinner—is a dim mirror of the Eucharistic meal that stands at the core of Christian practice. It involves sharing, eating and living relationships. In fact, artists have made much of a festive dinner spoiled (think of the heartbreaking, ruined Christmas dinner in James Joyce's novel *A Portrait of the Artist as a Young Man*) by the eruption of hatred or family argument. Eating beyond the need to provide oneself with nutrition is radically a communal event. A little test proves the point: think of the best meal you have ever had. Chances are, it was not a meal taken alone.

Among the seven deadly sins, gluttony alone is described as bringing in its wake both physical and psychological results noxious for human beings. In a curious reflection on gluttony, St. Thomas Aquinas defines gluttony as an "inordinate desire for food and drink" and says that it brings forth "five daughters": inappropriate pleasure, surliness, uncleanliness, stupidity, and *hebetudo mentis*, which may be understood roughly as mental slowness.

Dante, describing his exemplar of gluttony in the *Inferno*, notes that "Ciacco the Hog" stays stupefied on a pile of garbage with his head down and afflicted with strabismus (crossed eyes)—symptomatic, according to medieval medicine, for *hebetudo mentis*. William Langland, the writer of the allegorical narrative poem *Piers Plowman*, has a more vivid description:

> And to drink all days in di-
> verse taverns . . .
> to gobble food on fasting days
> before the fitting time,
> and then to sit supping until
> sleep assails them,
> and to grow portly as a town
> pig and to repose in soft beds
> Till sloth and sleep sleek their
> sides.

The constant stuffing of food and drink brings with it observable results: obesity, dullness, and the odd pleasure of eating for the sake of eating. Langland also notes that gluttony leads to another deadly sin: sloth. Of course, this ancient literature must be allowed its rhetorical excess, but what all these writers have in common is the conviction that gluttony has its consequences beyond lethal damage to the body.

Our media and our health-care workers are full of warnings about our contemporary obesity pandemic. They also point out consequences beyond getting fat, such as diabetes, heart problems, and other conditions. Obesity, diabetes, or high cholesterol, however, is not the same as gluttony, or even—if there is such a thing—"food addiction."

Many things have contributed to our national disease of obesity. They are constantly enumerated for us: our predilection for fast food; our penchant for sugar-laced soft drinks; our lost opportunities for actual physical work; our hunger for greasy food, coupled with our lack of enthusiasm for vegetables and fruit; the siren song of television advertising (think of the cereal ads aimed at children). In other words—and not to harp on the subject—obesity is a by-product of profound cultural shifts in a largely post-agricultural and postindustrial society. Lumberjacks may require four thousand calories a day, but store clerks, stockbrokers, and college professors do not. Obesity is, paradoxically, a symptom both of the rich (we can afford to eat whatever we want) and the poor (we eat lots of starch because it is cheap).

There is nothing wrong with taking pleasure at table, but the glutton separates out the pursuit of pleasure as fundamental with no reference to nutrition or conviviality. Gluttony is a solitary pursuit—a kind of alimentary self-abuse. What the ancient Christian tradition most objected to about gluttony was that it struck against common humanity with consequences for the individual and society. It is a sin and not merely an "addiction." A famous late-medieval painting by Hieronymus Bosch depicts the seven deadly sins. In portraying gluttony, Bosch has a corpulent man gorging himself at a table, while off to the side stands another man guzzling from a wine jug. The key to the painting, however, is a child fruitlessly pulling at the seated figure and begging for something to eat. Bosch's point is that the glutton is so preoccupied with his own needs that he cannot see the needs of another. That scene tells it all. It is a striking image of the old definition of the sinner: *incurvatus in se*— turned or curved inward on the self.

Gluttony's opposite is the virtue of temperance. All of us require a certain temperance with respect to food and drink, and, most often as a New Year's resolution, we pledge to be temperate, if for no other reason than good health. Given our ability to be globally aware, however, there is another good reason to resist excess and cultivate more awareness of how and what we eat: the rampant hunger in the world. It is fundamental to the teaching of Jesus that we turn to the other when we think of food. That Jesus fed the crowds at the multiplication of the loaves and fish (Mk 6) struck the gospel writers as so important that all four of them recorded the event. In his last great sermon on the end times recorded in Matthew's gospel (chapter 25), Jesus says that when we give food to the hungry we are, in effect, giving food to him. The Christian tradition has always, from its beginnings, taught that feeding the hungry is one of the great acts of mercy and justice. Jesus tells of the rich man and Lazarus in chapter 16 of the Gospel of Luke. It begins with the poor man fighting with dogs for scraps from the rich man's table. The unspoken point, of course, is that the rich man is a true villain in the story—completely indifferent to the plight of the poor.

Although the glutton may not be conscious of it (and, given his preoccupation for the self and its satisfactions, he would typically not be), the abuse and misuse of food, even for personal gratification, is an affront to the poor of the world. It would be wrong, then, to look at gluttony solely in terms of the harm that it does to the individual. Food is, in a radical fashion, a social reality. The teaching of the contemporary Buddhist teacher Thich Nhat Hanh, who argues that all humans must learn mindfulness, has always impressed me. He says that we need to cultivate awareness of where our food comes from, learn who has produced it for us, and, finally, be mindful of those who have no food. That sentiment is similar to one that the early medieval monk Alcuin of York prayed: "Whenever we eat we should give thanks to You. And having received from your hands, let us give with equally generous hands to

To order rightly our eating and drinking is not only an exercise of temperance but also a profoundly Christian act. St. Paul reaches for the metaphor of food to make the point that the right use of food (and he has in mind, especially, the Eucharist) has profound implications that involve both our common humanity and our bonds with the risen Lord: "Because the loaf of bread is one, we, though many, are one body, for we all partake of the one loaf" (1 Cor 10:17).

TWO

SOME PURE THOUGHTS
ON LUST

Immorality or any impurity . . . must not even
be mentioned among you. . . .

EPHESIANS 5:3

Is it odd that the late Wallace Stevens (1879–1955), a but-
toned-up insurance executive from Hartford, Connecticut,
is numbered among the finest modernist American poets?
He was anything but the stereotype of the bohemian artist. Stevens did not even publish poetry until he was in his
mid forties and already settled in his business career as an
executive. However, he was a great poet. His poem "Peter
Quince at the Clavier" is, to my mind, the single greatest
expression of human sexual desire written in our time. Stevens weaves into the poem the biblical story (Dn 13:1–63)
of Susanna and the elders. Susanna, an innocent wife, is
bathing—unaware that some supposedly righteous elders
are spying on her. Burning with lust for her, they attempt

to rape her. Susanna rebuffs them, and, for revenge, the elders falsely accuse her of adultery with another man, only to have their deceit uncovered by the wise interrogation of the prophet Daniel.

Here is Stevens on the "red-eyed" elders, who felt "the basses of their beings throb / In witching chords and their thin blood / Pulse pizzicati of Hosanna." Toward the end of the poem, the poet will tell how the music of Susanna "touched the bawdy strings" of the elders. The poem, replete with music, desire, and depictions of the voyeuristic elders, embodies the experience of lust. The "red-eyed elders" not only felt a lascivious desire for the innocent Susanna but, thwarted, desired revenge by accusing Susanna of having an illicit sexual encounter with a young man. It is worthy to note that to prove adultery in Jewish law (a crime punishable through death by stoning in the ancient code) there had to be witnesses, so their perjury would bring down a death sentence on Susanna based on the strength of their (false) witness. The elders were not only lustful but perjurers to boot. One sin easily leads to another.

Most commonly identified with insistently illicit sexual desire, lust is associated by most people with words like bawdy, lecherous, lascivious, carnal, and so on. The British writer Dorothy Sayers, in an address she gave early in World War II, classed lust, along with gluttony and wrath, as a "warm sin" because it is derived from the body for the sake of physical pleasure and somewhat free from rational reflection. These sins stand in contrast to the "cold" sins of envy and pride, which are located in the mind and heart.

St. Augustine's *Confessions* details his attempt to overcome his powerful sexual urges and his weakness in that attempt. Looking back on his youth, Augustine famously recalled that "as a youth I had prayed to you for chastity and said 'Give me chastity and continence but not just yet' for I was fearful that you would answer my prayer at once and cure me too soon of the disease of lust which I wanted satisfied not quelled" (VIII:7). It is not only a rhetorical point that Augustine makes when his eyes fall on a particular text in St. Paul at the time of his dramatic conversion, when he picks up a codex of Paul's letters in the garden and he reads: ". . . not in revelry and drunkenness, not in debauchery and licentiousness, not in quarreling and jealousy but instead put on the Lord Jesus Christ and make no provision for the flesh, to gratify its desires" (Rom 13:13–14). In reading the *Confessions*, we learn that Augustine insists on the point that the lust he experienced controlled him until he was capable of controlling it. So powerful was this drive in Augustine that, as we follow his story, it is clear that Augustine overcame his intellectual problems with the claims of the Christian faith before he could rein in his lustful appetites in practice.

However, we should hasten to add that the word "lust" has a far more complicated history behind it than sexual desire, even though it is common enough to equate sexual desire with lust. In truth, sexual urges are part of normal human experience, and, as such, bear no hint of sin in and of themselves.

We might begin by considering how the word is used in our everyday discourse. We speak of "blood lust" or a "lust for life" or "wanderlust," or describe an exuberant extroverted person who "lets the good times roll" as leading a lusty life. What rests behind all those common phrases is the concept of an intense appetite or a driving desire. It is only by extension that we narrow the term down to speak of lust as inordinate sexual desire. It is interesting that the Latin term for lust is *luxuria*, which means riotous or excessive behavior. Think of our use of the term "luxury goods," which speaks of lavish excess, rather than those goods that are necessary, useful, or merely sufficient. Standard English dictionaries typically provide the meaning "strong desire" as lust's first meaning and inordinate sexual desire as the second meaning. I suspect that too often we move to the second meaning without paying attention to the first.

Lust is not only numbered as one of the deadly sins but, by most counts, begins the list. In an extremely interesting passage in St. John's first letter, we find a compressed list that speaks of illicit desire: "If anyone loves the world, the Father is not in him. For all that is in the world, sensual lust, enticement of the eye, a pretentious life, is not from the Father but from the world" (1 Jn 2:15–16). Thus, for St. John, inordinate desire or lust can dwell in the flesh sensually or in the eye invidiously or in the self as pride. In all these cases, the emphasis is on inordinate interior desire, as Jesus himself pointed out when he famously noted that a man who looks lustfully at a woman has already committed adultery in his heart (Mt 5:27–28).

In the order of the seven deadly sins, lust is viewed as the least sinful. Jesus is less condemnatory relative to public sinners, such as prostitutes, than he is with religious hypocrites. Dante condemns the hopelessly lustful in the first circle of hell and purges the forgiven lustful in the final terrace of purgatory. The Christian moralists tended to think of lust as reflecting animal instincts, whereas malice was only possible for the sinfully rational mind; lust is "warm," to borrow Dorothy Sayers's nice division, while malice is "cold." In other words, lust is a twisting of a base instinct, and typically free of the cold intellectual calculation of other sins. It is not puritanical to note that much modern advertising and much in modern culture is designed precisely to trigger lust due to its close connection to our instincts for survival. Of course, sins like murder, betrayal, or revenge may well be rationalized and planned out, but the generic form of "road rage," so common today, erupts with little thought and much passion, just as does sexual scheming.

The traditional remedies for lust include "custody of the eyes," self-discipline, fasting (spicy foods were thought to engender lust), prayer, and disciplined activity. Such remedies were thought to "contain" these instincts. If John's first letter outlines broad categories of lust, St. Thomas Aquinas sets lust squarely in the context of the deadly sins but, understands lust primarily as a sexual sin. In nineteen different places in the *Summa Theologiae*, he discusses lust. What catches my eye is his analysis of how lust arises in the human heart: lust begins in "looking," and then moves to mulling over, enjoyment, internal consent, and final action. Without analyzing these various stages, which are not always as finely distinguished as Aquinas would suggest, lust is first of all internal, which, when occasion affords, erupts into lustful activity.

Thomas, by the way, cribbed his analysis of the progression of desire from earlier monastic analyses of the struggle against lust for the tempted monk and notes that the deadly sins all have intimate interconnections. He says that lust arises from *acedia*—that lazy listlessness called the "noonday devil." To put it in contemporary language, the best antidote for lust is not to let time hang heavily and uselessly on your hands.

What Aquinas analyzes somewhat methodically is something that every healthy person experiences frequently (and often haphazardly) when our basic drives, which arise from our biological makeup, are triggered by either some external stimulus or from the storehouse of our individual memories. Such drives operate at different levels. Like all other drives within us, there is nothing wrong in desiring more money, more honor, to find an attractive mate, in being stirred sensually at the sight of a beautiful person, and so on. It is only sinful when such desires control us, rather than we controlling them.

Let us reiterate that the sexual drive in humans is a positive good. The person who is asexual is often thought of as incomplete, and anyone who would give up the right to sexual activity because it is evil or dirty is not a Christian, but a Gnostic. After all, the high value the Catholic tradition places on virginity or the celibate life is done so, not because sexuality is bad, but precisely because it is good and worthy to be given up for the higher good of serving the Christian community. Pope Benedict, in his encyclical on love (*Deus Caritas Est*, "God is Love"), argues strenuously that erotic love leads to self-giving love precisely because erotic love—the physical love for another—is not disordered.

Dante makes a subtle point in the terrace of the lustful in the *Purgatorio*. Those purging away the effects of lust walk around the terrace enveloped in sheets of fire, but as they pass each other they exchange the biblical kiss of peace. They can make that carnal gesture, for it is done from pure motives quite distant from the passions that brought them to this last purgative stage of the mountain in the first place. It is only after this final stage of purgation that the eyes of the penitents are cleansed, and they are ready to move to the earthly paradise—and from there, to the heavenly spheres.

What the Christian tradition at its best has insisted is that unbridled lust not infrequently bursts out from the confines of one's internal urges to activities that are personally degrading or are injurious to society in general (sex slavery), or to persons in particular (child sexual abuse, rape, etc.). By contrast, the sexual attraction of men to women and women to men is not only wholesome but a positive good sacramentally recognized in matrimony.

Lust may be such an old-fashioned word that it no longer has the punch to provide a warning about its evil. More's the pity. It is so commonplace to see everything sexualized in the various media that it is difficult to see clearly the destructive ends to which sexuality may be directed. Perhaps we might suggest a question in the form of a test: how does one distinguish attractive love from lust? Or, to put it another way: when does that physical attraction one feels for a close friend or one we admire or one we care deeply for turn from love into lust? One answer to that question is this: lust enters into the heart when the object of lust is just that—an *object* and not a person. In that sense, lust is about me and not the other person. It is that first step toward the sin that brought down the angels: self-absorbing pride.

Now, it is undoubtedly the case that historically the Catholic Church has fiercely preached against sexual sin, perhaps to the point of denigrating sexuality in the process (Pope Benedict XVI himself admits this in *Deus Caritas Est*). It is also the case that the contemporary clergy, by and large, has not been as ferocious in denouncing sexual sin as it has in the past. At the same time, we should not pass over the issue of lust in our society. Let us, in fact, argue that unbridled allowance of lust is a parlous condition exhibited in contemporary society.

The proof of the above assertion is not too hard to find. The most degrading forms of pornography are instantly accessible on the Internet. The sexual abuse of children has been front-page news in almost every country. While such crimes are crimes of violence and misuse of power, this does not mean that they are free of lust. The trafficking of women as sexual slaves is a persistent worldwide problem for authorities. Marital infidelity is blithely discussed in the media and exhibited by "celebrities"; and sexual innuendo is as commonplace on the stage and screen as jokes about the weather. We are all aware of the phenomenon of "sexting" (the sending of lascivious messages or photos over social media) among the young and the sad consequences that come from such activities.

What must be remembered when thinking about these instances and others like them is that the gratification of the instinct of lust is not free from the lust for money or from the lust for power. After all, is it not a commonplace that sexually motivated acts of aggression—especially against women—are nothing more than a show of power driven by the desire for mastery? Thus, rape is less a "warm" sin of sexuality and more a sin of violence; rapists typically want to exhibit power and, more specifically, the power to degrade. Finally, the fruits of lust result in the degradation of others—turning them from persons who have a right to dignity in their own personhood into objects who satisfy "needs." The basic evil of pornography is not in its exhibitionism but in that it never satisfies the voyeur—which explains why, paradoxically, pornography is both boring and addictive; it is a species of gluttony that always promises *more*. The pornographic subject is an object (not a person), and the pornographic act is mechanical, but neither loving nor authentically human.

A final note: lust is essentially a turning in on the self. In one of his wonderful essays on the seven deadly sins, the late political journalist and social critic Henry Fairlie made an extremely interesting point that deserves quotation: "Pornographic literature and movies do not incite us to strenuous emulations. On the contrary, they are substitutes, evidence not of the strength of our sexual feelings, but of their enfeeblement. . . . It is a substitute again for involvement with another person."[2]

It is the rare person who is not tempted to lust over food or drink or sexual activity or any of those myriad impulses that can overwhelm a person. In fact, is it not the case that twelve-step programs have flourished in our own day to rein in everything from overeating to addiction to pornography? Alcoholics Anonymous has adopted as its unofficial prayer the serenity prayer ascribed to the late theologian Reinhold Niebuhr ("God grant me the serenity to accept the things I cannot change / the courage to change the things I cannot / and the wisdom to know the difference."), but few understand that the prayer ends with a more overtly Christian coda that insists a person acknowledge the sinful nature of his or her life and the need for supernatural aid. The prayer ends with words with which everyone can make an appeal as we struggle with any or all of our inordinate desires:

> Taking, as he did, this sinful
> world
> As it is, not as I would have it;
> Trusting that he will make all
> things right
> If I surrender to his will;
> That I may be reasonably
> happy in this life
> And supremely happy with him
> Forever in the next. Amen.

The key words, of course, are "surrender to his will" because, as scripture teaches us so clearly, God never tempts us beyond our capacity to resist. That surrender comes with the powerful presence of God's grace shaping our

THREE

SOME GENEROUS THOUGHTS ON GREED

Scrooge . . . was hard and sharp as flint, from which no steel
had struck out generous fire; secret, and self-contained, and
as solitary as an oyster.

CHARLES DICKENS, *A CHRISTMAS CAROL*

We would be well served to begin a discussion of greed
with a reflection on the Ten Commandments. The first
three commandments deal with our relationship to God,
while the next seven treat of humans in relationship with
each other. The last two—on not coveting another's wife
or another person's goods (Ex 20:17)—are rather singu-
lar for two reasons. First, they are the only commandments that forbid an interior disposition rather than an act.
Second, the notion of "coveting" someone or something
seems, when viewed minimally, only a kind of innocent
envy. The truth is that "coveting person or thing" is, as one
commentator put it, "action in rehearsal."

What is forbidden in those last commandments is the act of scheming to take over what is not one's own. Under the prohibition would be forms of personal fraud or unjust confiscation. The prohibition to covet, in short, is a law that prohibits unjust plans of aggrandizement in order to acquire "more" in an unjust fashion. The social reality behind those commandments is the conviction that no community or society can function harmoniously if the unbridled greed of one is not somehow bridled. The *Catechism* puts it bluntly: "The tenth commandment forbids greed and the desire to amass earthly goods without limit. It forbids *avarice* arising from the passion for riches and their attendant power. It also forbids the desire to commit injustice by harming our neighbor in his temporal goods" (*CCC*, 2536).

It is interesting to note that St. Thomas Aquinas found the sin of avarice (greed) as one of the worst of the seven deadly sins because of its dynamic capacity to engender other sins (see *Summa* II II, 118.5). The American writer and philosopher James Ogilvy provides a precise explanation of why Aquinas is correct: "Greed turns love into lust, leisure into sloth, hunger into gluttony, honor into pride, righteous indignation into anger, and admiration into envy. If it weren't for greed, we'd suffer fewer of the other vices."[3]

Obviously, the Christian tradition sees greed as a sin that always refers to the self. Such egomania makes it almost impossible to focus away from the self and its possessions toward God. The English martyr Margaret Clitherow (1556–1586) was pressed to death on Good Friday in 1586 because she refused to be interrogated about her Catholic life in the city of York during the Elizabethan period that made being a Catholic a high crime. Of her non-Catholic husband who loved her (and she him), Margaret once re-marked that he found it hard to raise his eyes to God be-cause he was so bowed down by his worldly goods. Such a person, as St. John Cassian says pithily in his *Institutes*, "fixes his intellect on the love, not of God, but of the im-ages of men stamped on gold coins."

The good Anglo-Saxon word "greed" was almost a syn-onym for hunger when it was first used. Greed, in that sense, described how a hungry person wolfed down food. By extension, it became a word that described excessive hunger for food or an inordinate desire for drink. In our modern vocabulary, it is most commonly used to charac-terize an excessive desire for material goods in general and money in particular and, by extension, ravenousness for intangibles like praise. The word carried with it the ex-tended meaning of insatiable desire. "Greed is good," said Gordon Gekko in the film *Wall Street*, because "it works," and in his judgment "raises all boats." That Oliver Stone wrote the script should lead us to the conclusion that the film did not agree with that famous line. Greed is not good.

As it was listed among the seven deadly sins, greed was known by the Latinate word "avarice" (*avaritia*), which

THE SEVEN DEADLY SINS

has always meant an excessive impulse to hoard money or the goods money affords or more simply to hunger for more and more inordinately. The miser, of course, is greed's stereotypic character, and rare is the occasion when anyone portrays a sympathetic miser. Indeed, as the conversion of Ebenezer Scrooge in Dickens's *A Christmas Carol* demonstrates so famously, it is the repentance of the miser that is most frequently held up as an ideal. Similarly, Molière's play *The Miser* is a drama of morality set in comedic terms with the miser (*l'avare*) as the butt of the more generous characters' jokes.

However, equating avarice with the miser would miss the point. Becoming a miser is only the extreme outcome of avarice. The Christian moralists have always seen avarice, like gluttony and lust, as sins of excess. The person who is avaricious turns a good thing—the need for goods to sustain oneself—into a drive to possess more and more for no other end than to possess. In that sense, avarice is a constant bending inward toward the self. It is no wonder, then, that the opposite of avarice, in our traditional catechism, is generosity—the virtue by which we give rather than receive or acquire. After all, St. Paul does not say that money is "the root of all evils"; it is the love of money (1 Tm 6:10) that causes people to stray from the faith.

In Canto VII of the *Inferno*, Dante and his guide Virgil come to the circle where the Prodigal and the Avaricious roll great boulders in a never-ending circle. Dante is quick

to note that among the greedy are many who wear the ton-
sure of clerics, as well as a goodly number of high prel-
ates, including cardinals and popes. Dante's linking of
the sin of avarice with the clergy is a very old trope in
Christian literature from antiquity. The Church has always
been plagued by people who take advantage of their ex-
alted roles for purposes of self-aggrandizement and the
accumulation of riches. Indeed, St. Augustine of Hippo,
centuries before Dante, discussing the place of widows in
the Church, wrote—perhaps thinking of the celibates of
his own day—that it was his observation, "this fact of human behavior that, with certain people, when sexuality is
repressed avarice seems to grow in its place."

St. Thomas Aquinas taught that the precise sinfulness of
avarice consists in the rational and sinful judgment of
someone who considers the acquisition of temporal goods
to be preferable to eternal goods. What makes avarice sinful is that the greedy person makes the object of his or her
desires the end point of the will. The avaricious person
chooses limited goods over eternal goods. Implicit in that
insight is the very testable proposition that temporal goods
are, by definition, temporal. Folk wisdom understands that
truth in its proverbial insistence that "you cannot take it
with you."

Death is the definitive cure for avarice. Jesus tells a very
powerful story illustrating the point. He imagines a very
rich man who had the good fortune of bringing in (or more

precisely, having his slaves bring in) a fabulous harvest. The sheer abundance of the harvest drove him to tear down his granaries and barns to build larger ones for storage. So pleased with himself, he thinks that he is so secure in his accumulated goods that he can "take his ease" and "eat, drink and be merry." The story ends with these words: "Fool! This night your soul is required of you; and the things you have prepared, whose will they be?" Jesus then drives home the point by saying, "So is he who lays up treasure for himself and is not rich towards God" (Lk 12:16–21).

Jesus introduces that well-known parable in the Gospel of Luke with the unadorned warning: "Take heed and beware of all covetousness, for a human life does not consist in the abundance of his possessions" (Lk 12:15). In that same chapter, Jesus goes on to make a further point in a polemic against greed: "Make purses for yourselves that do not wear out, an unfailing treasure in heaven, where no thief comes near and no moth destroys. *For where your treasure is, there your heart will be also*" (Lk 12:33–34; my emphasis). On more than one occasion in these pages we will return to that brilliant observation, namely to ask, what does the heart most treasure?

When greed is considered at its most extreme, what Jesus said is empirically true. We have noted already that the miser is always thought of as miserable; indeed, the two words have a common origin. To repeat a point made in other contexts in these essays: the radical turn to the self and its demands will cause, in the end, self-destruction.

How are we to understand the truth of what Jesus says about the temporality of possessions when we think about a culture in which hedonism and material display are held up as something to which we should aspire? Is it true, as the bumper sticker says, that he who has the most toys wins? Is it the case that the golden rule is that the one who has the gold makes the rules? When we live in a society where the basic necessities of shelter, material sustenance, health care, and education are assumed (shelter your eyes from the homeless, the food banks, and the unemployment lines in your town as you read!), when do the markers of success or "the good life" become excessive? Or is it the case if you are a materialist that slackness in the acquisition of "more" is a fault or a sign of a lack of get-up-and-go? Is it not the case that those who drown in credit card debt find themselves in that situation precisely because they thought foolishly that the acquisition of more goods would guarantee them a happy and successful life?

A wise bishop in a homily once said that the plight of the poor is a perennial concern of the Church, but in our society the new problem the excesses of the rich or, at least, the temptations faced by the flaunting of the rich who, as it was once said of the Bourbons, know the price of everything but the value of nothing.

Our tendency is to think of avarice as a temptation for the individual, but greed can also be a communal fault. We may not think of it as a sin, but we can let ourselves be so concerned with our own well-being that we implicitly become greedy for "me" or "us" at the expense of the other. We have already noted that it is the turning in on the self that gives precise character to the so-called deadly sins.

When greed is understood more communally, we can quiz ourselves both as individuals and communities with questions like these. Am I so greedy for powerful cars that I blissfully consume fossil fuels without a thought about the natural world in which I live? Am I so accustomed to cheap fruits and vegetables that I am indifferent to the stooped labor that produces our abundance? Will I cooperate in the devouring of farmland in order to live in a McMansion? Does my self-esteem demand that, debt be damned, my entertainment center be bigger, my vacations more exotic, my clothing come only in designer brands, my portfolio include dubious holdings? Do we pay any attention at all to the fact that our reasonably priced clothing comes from the hard labor of fourth-world factory slaves who barely eke out a living?

When we begin to ask questions like these, the once-avaricious individual grubbing for money turns complicit in a larger scene, thus becoming an issue of social justice. Behind the pleas of the Church in its social encyclicals for a more equitable sharing of goods with the world, careful readers will detect warnings about the sin of avarice. Consumerism in its extreme manifestation becomes contemporary coinage for avarice.

In response to the assumption that profits come before people, the Church insists, "Human activity is for the benefit of human beings, proceeding from them as it does. When they work, not only do they transform matter and society, they also perfect themselves. . . . Rightly understood, this kind of growth is more precious than any kind of wealth that can be amassed" (*Gaudium et Spes*, 35). Not to put too fine a point on it—the sin of avarice is not simply the sin of the miser; it is a force against which the social teaching of the Church is alert.

What is the remedy for avarice? St. Thomas Aquinas says that its opposite virtue is something he calls *liberalitas*—a virtue we might call "generosity." At the heart of that Latin word is the idea of freedom. In other words, the generous person is not bound ultimately to his or her goods; the person of liberality gives or shares rather than being one who only, and unremittingly, acquires. The traditional expression of *liberalitas* is almsgiving, but we could easily extend it to mean care of our material goods for the common good, generosity with time for the sake of the other, a certain asceticism with respect to luxury, a keen sense of our debt to those who are poor, enough wisdom to distinguish "enough" from "too much," an understanding that we should possess our goods rather than having the goods possess us. As Peter Maurin, the cofounder of the Catholic Worker Movement, once said, the extra coat hanging in the closet belongs to the poor.

When considering the weight of the sin of greed, it is worthwhile to remember what a careful reading of the Bible shows. Contrary to what many may think, the scripture writers spend far less time discussing the sins of sex and much more time writing on the dangers of money and possessions. This is as true in the writings of the prophets as it is in the preaching of Jesus. One way in which the New Testament shows us this truth is in its very concreteness. It has been wisely observed that the Bible does not speak about poverty, but it has much to say about the poor. It warns against putting burdens on the poor. It strikes out at those who have no heed for the needs of others. It relativizes wealth (think of the costly perfume anointing Jesus); it reacts in horror that someone would betray Jesus for a bag of silver; it sees Jesus in the hungry, thirsty, naked, and homeless. The preaching of Jesus is in line with the ethical monotheism of the great eighth-century prophets.

Let us make a final theological point. The avaricious turn in on themselves in their insatiable grasp for "more." By contrast, the entire story of Trinitarian theology is one of giving and pouring forth. The Trinitarian dynamic in time is one of giving first in creation and then in history and finally in the Word made flesh (Jn 1:14). Prodigality in giving frames the entire story of salvation. The old Fathers of the Church, in describing God, often used the philosophical axiom that the "good diffuses itself." Everything we have from creation—where we live, our very being, our final destiny, and our full relationship with God in Christ—comes to us as *pure gift*, from that liberality that we call grace. Indeed, creation itself, freely given by the Creator, is itself a gift: we cannot claim that creation is due to us. That liberality has been summed up in a lyrical passage that opens Paul's letter to the Church at Ephesus: "Blessed be the God and Father of Our Lord Jesus Christ, who has blessed us in Christ with every spiritual blessing in the heavenly places just as he chose us in Christ before the foundation of the world to be holy and blameless before him in love. He destined us for the adoption as his children through Jesus Christ, according to the good pleasure of his will, to the praise of his glorious grace that he has bestowed on us in the Beloved" (Eph 1:3–6).

FOUR

SOME FOCUSED
THOUGHTS ON SLOTH

Go to the ant, O sluggard, study her ways and learn wisdom!

PROVERBS 6:6

I began reading about the sin of sloth last summer prior to writing these thoughts, which is appropriate enough, because in the modern vocabulary sloth is almost a synonym for laziness. Who is not tempted, in the hot, languid days of July, to forget work and laze about in the shade with a cool drink? Who does not prize a good nap? Who does not point the finger at the "workaholic" while suggesting that such a person take a break? The Italians have a word about such innocent dawdling about; they call it the *dolce far niente*, which means, literally, "sweet do nothing," by which they mean a kind of leisurely rest (like a good siesta!) or a bit of messing around as an antidote to the busyness of life.

One could make an argument that leisure is essential for human thriving. I remember well a comment once made by a Notre Dame commencement speaker who told graduates that they should acquire a space for leisure. The speaker concluded that no one in the history of the world ever said on his deathbed that he wished he had spent more time in the office.

Dolce far niente has nothing to do with sloth. Indeed, one could argue that it is a virtuous way of spending some time in order to enhance the happiness of life. After all, it is a principle that comes to us from antiquity that quiet rest (*otium*) is needed for culture to thrive. But however much we allow for a little recreational laziness, we nonetheless can work up heated moral sermons when laziness becomes a way of life. We thunder against those who are too lazy to do a good day's work. Our vocabulary is rife with unflattering words to describe those who do not manifest the "virtue" of industry, hard work, and pulling oneself up by the bootstraps; to such we use the damning vocabulary of shiftlessness, worthlessness, and other derogatory terms. Such screeds against laziness are stock and trade in our contemporary political discourse—especially when the subject of welfare comes up.

There is much to be said about putting in a good day's work. It is a theme to which I return often when faced with the too-frequent excuses from my students about readings not done, papers not written, tardiness in getting to class on time, and absences from lectures. I often cite the words of Blessed John Henry Newman, who once said that the secret of Christian perfection is to get up in the morning, pray, get in a day's duties, finish with sensible recreation, recite one's night prayers, and get to bed on time. A much briefer summary of Newman's advice comes from the old Jesuit motto *age quod agis*—do what you are supposed to be doing.

Constant diligence is challenging, and we all have our moments of slacking. (Sometimes those moments are just signs that we are too busy for our own good.) But when the Christian tradition talks about the deadly sin of sloth, it has in mind more than a bit of neglectful goofing off. Real sloth has to do with a deeper, spiritual dimension of the sin rather than the mere surface meaning of lack of diligence.

First, we should understand that sloth is not to be confused with leisure. In fact, the ancients praised leisure as essential for the serious person. Years ago, Josef Pieper wrote a little book titled *Leisure: The Basis of Culture.* Pieper's point was that some freedom from the grind of making a living is essential if plays are to be written, music composed, statues carved, and sensible political philosophy created. One requires time and space in order to work creatively. To put a more personal spin on it, that kind of leisure is critical for the scholar who needs, above all, free time.

We should also understand that leisure does not mean frantic activity that falls under the name of "fun" or "vacation" or "day off" as an alternative to work. Here is a curious oxymoron: "leisure industry." That term reflects the peculiarly American penchant for making a dollar from what should be free. We buy all sorts of things, from motor homes to equipment, so as to enjoy "leisure," without ever considering that we may be consuming in order to avoid real quiet and reflection. True leisure, as Pieper understood the term, is a kind of quiet recollection and a form of human rest. The late Trappist monk Matthew Kelty once said that when retreatants come to the monastery, a good portion of them sleep for most of the first day because people do not realize how exhausted they really are.

The early monks took over the idea of leisure from the pagan past and spoke lovingly of the necessity for *sacrum otium*: a "holy leisure" required for those who lead the contemplative life. One must have time to read, meditate, and pray. Thomas Merton understood this perfectly. He often complained in his journals that monks were too busy to become true contemplatives. He often found his own monastery a beehive of work and labor when what was more needed was time for contemplative recollection.

The early commentators considered sloth to be a vice and not merely a bad use of time. Early Christian commentators often invoked the line from Psalm 90:6 (in the Vulgate version) about the "noonday devil" to describe it. What they meant by sloth (or, as they called it, *acedia*) was that inner lassitude in which the person gives up the pursuit of the good or virtuous life by becoming overwhelmed with a kind of listlessness that makes effort unattractive at best or, at worst, impossible. The "noonday devil" was understood to be like that fatigue that comes over one at midday, sapping strength and resolve.

It was frequently the case that the early commentators saw sloth as verging on a kind of quiet despair. St. Cassian, in his *Institutes*, gives examples of this despairing restlessness that infects the lives of monks: looking at the sun to see if it is time to eat, killing time by wandering about to meet other monks to see if there is any good gossip, the persistent temptation to daydream about moving to another monastery where conditions are better and life more attractive. At the heart of this sloth is an inner turmoil combining restlessness, lack of will, inability to continue the daily round, wild imaginings of another kind of life, and a brooding inability to stay the course. Sloth is a paralysis of the will to continue. Thomas Aquinas observed that sloth of this sort engendered "hatred of work." Sloth begins in dissatisfaction and ends in desperation. The slothful person no longer sees a goal in life. While the Christian fathers considered sloth to be both a sin and an ailment, it is important to separate the vice of sloth from the illness of depression. They are second cousins, certainly, but not synonymous. It should be further noted—if it needs noting!—that depression is not a sin; it is an ailment.

Sloth in the Christian tradition has often been seen as a kind of weariness that invades the whole person. But, most especially, it is a weariness that erodes the willingness to cultivate the Christian life of virtue and practice. It is a phenomenon, shed of its spiritual overtones, common enough in contemporary society, but we tend to use a different vocabulary to describe it: restlessness, apathy, the "blues," dissatisfaction, or malaise. It is that deep-seated state of mind that infects a person who is bored out of his skull at work, who regards future prospects as slim to none, who finds home life tedious. Such a state often gives rise to an internal monologue best captured in a single judgment that one's life is without meaning. It is then that the temptation rears its head in any number of implausible fantasies, such as running away to live on the beach in Hawaii or, more worryingly, simply giving up and going through the motions. The contemporary spiritual writer and poet Kathleen Norris (in her book *Acedia & Me*, to which we will return) has brilliantly described this temptation to spiritual sloth, which, as she has observed, can afflict those who prize self-motivation or who are in it "for the long haul" (think of marriage!).

In the *Purgatorio*, Dante equates sloth with the unwillingness to pursue the good as one should; sloth, in that sense, is a failure of duty. Not surprisingly, the purgatorial punishment for penitents is to "make haste"—to run around the terraces of the Mount of Purgatory as a countersign to their sloth in life. Commentators point out that these penitents alone do not utter a prayer or a liturgical hymn and will not do so until they have been purged of their sloth. At this point they just cannot make the effort. Dante contends that zeal is the virtue to be acquired to replace the vice of sloth. Mary, who made haste to visit her cousin Elizabeth (Lk 1:39), is held up as the great biblical exemplum for those who run in expiation on the fourth terrace of the Mount of Purgatory.

Acedia has recently been given a full-length treatment in a wonderful book by the contemporary essayist, poet, and spiritual writer Kathleen Norris: *Acedia & Me* (Riverhead/ Penguin, 2008). Norris says that it was in reading the early monastic literature that she first learned how to name something that afflicted her from her adolescent years: a sense of restlessness bookended between periods of sheer apathy and frenetic busyness. She tells her story in tandem with a memoir of her thirty-year marriage, which ended in widowhood, and her own career as a professional writer.

Norris offers the salutary advice that one kind of medicine against spiritual sloth is care for others, since such acts, of necessity, take one away from too much concern for the self. It is sage advice, since the care for others almost by definition means turning away from one's own needs in order to aid the other. She recommends reciting the Lord's Prayer as a way to battle *acedia* by staying grounded in the present day.

Norris goes on to offer the advice of monastic writer Evagrius of Pontus: "What heals *acedia* is staunch persistence. . . . Decide upon a set amount for yourself, in every work, and do not turn aside from it before you complete it." When battling her tendency toward sloth, Norris says she starts small and tackles humble activities, thereby accepting life's limitations and battling grandiose distractions. She adds that it is hard to accept that we find meaning and fulfillment "by starting where we are, not where we would like to be." Norris sees this as an antidote to what the writer Henry David Thoreau once called the "quiet despair" that afflicts so many people. If one wishes to find empirical evidence that this kind of sloth is exactly as Norris has described it, one need look no further than in the thriving industry of motivational seminars and very rich motivational speakers who promise, for a fee, to put back into one's person his old zip and go.

In his treatment of the "seven deadly sins," St. Thomas Aquinas views sloth as fundamentally a religious issue. He characterizes *acedia* as a kind of spiritual sadness in relation to belief and practice. As such, he places sloth in opposition to charity, for, he comments, we should find joy in the life of faith, and such joy generates love. The polar opposite of sloth is joy. That insight of Aquinas is brilliant, because the test of detecting the affliction of the slothful person is this: is his or her life joyless and bleak?

By contrast, not only does sloth oppose charity, it generates what Aquinas calls six daughters: malice, rancor, flabbiness of spirit, desperation, torpor, and an "unfocussed mind." Now, it is true that the medieval masters loved categories and lists if only for precision's sake. But anyone who looks at Aquinas's list will see quickly that he has made a list of symptoms that afflict, not only those seeking holiness consciously, but many contemporaries who find themselves (to borrow a phrase from the late novelist Walker Percy) sunk in "everydayness" and unable to figure out why they are so sad. While such problems may be hard to pinpoint, it may be wise to consider how the old ascetics and monks understood them almost reflexively. It is also worthwhile underscoring that Percy, himself a Catholic convert, saw his faith as a powerful antidote to the apparent meaninglessness of much of contemporary life.

A good argument could be made that sloth (*acedia*) is one of the premier vices that either tempt or afflict us moderns. A profound restlessness that makes us unhappy or blue or listless or aimless or restless or dissatisfied (pick your descriptions!) seems almost risible in an age when we are well fed and housed and given opportunity. Nonetheless, such is the case. If it were not, how do we explain the booming business in counseling, psychotherapy, and other such practices that blossom in our society? Why do drug companies do such a flourishing trade in mood boosters and tranquillizers? Do most people, as Thoreau observed in the nineteenth century, live lives of "quiet desperation"?

If this is the case, then, that which we often name some-thing else (boredom, a midlife crisis) is exactly what the old monks called *acedia* or sloth.

The remedies of such modern manifestations of *acedia* are incremental, ranging from religious convictions to practi-cal exercises. There is, it seems clear, some kind of con-nection between *acedia* or sloth and what is often called "loss of self-esteem." First, we are all children of God and infinitely precious in God's eyes—we are worthy, and not worthless. Next, who we are and what we do and how we live in this world is precious before God unless it is sin-ful. Third, every worthy thing we do and act and perform is virtuous in the eyes of God—thus, little steps of living mindfully are good things in themselves. We all have a purpose, and we all have an end—each step in living our lives is a bulwark against *acedia*. Finally, and for this we should give a nod to Kathleen Norris, one remedy for sloth is to find a way to be of help to another person—to break out from the self-imposed weariness of our own lives by forgetting our own self long enough to reach out to another.

FIVE

SOME JOYFUL
THOUGHTS ON ENVY

The infernal serpent; he it was whose guile stirred up with
envy and revenge, deceived the mother of mankind.

JOHN MILTON, *PARADISE LOST*

There is a persistent folk belief among some Mediterra-
nean peoples that envy is an almost palpable kind of malign force in the world. Envy appears when good fortune
befalls someone. It was believed to be so strong that strategies appeared to ward off its power. In rural Greece or Ita-
ly, it was considered bad form or even dangerous to praise
the beauty of a baby, lest "envy" snatch it. Many homes
would post an effigy of an all-seeing eye "to keep envy
away." Others wore amulets to ward off envy. This somewhat crude form of envy posits an unspoken belief that
there is something deep in human relations in which the
good fortune of one brings forth a malign urge to destroy
that good fortune in another.

Envy, in that sense, was a destructive force very different from what we mean when we use the term today. We might admit to envying a neighbor's new Lexus or express envy at the good luck of someone who won the lottery. Those uses, typically, are casual, conversational, and harmless. Even in casual conversation, someone might say something like "I envy her," or "He was the envy of everyone in the room." Such expressions are more akin to simple jealousy than venomous envy. The use of "envy" in the examples cited above has flattened out the deep meaning of the word.

Why, then, did Pope Gregory the Great slip envy into his list of the seven deadly sins? Why did he see it as part of a chain springing from pride, the mother lode of sins, since it did not appear in the list of *logismoi* coming from the older monastic tradition?

Why did Church Fathers, who thought deeply about envy at a time when people took the capital sins more seriously than they may today, see in it something destructive to one's humanity? A clue may be found in an observation of Thomas Aquinas. He describes envy as sadness (*tristitia*) at the goods possessed by another. Aquinas does not think that envy is some kind of elemental force but, rather, a corruption of the human tendency to experience sadness. The specific kind of sadness embedded in the Latin word *tristitia* carries with it a complex tone of suppressed rage, melancholy, and festering resentment directed at another.

Aquinas thought the demons experienced envy, and many centuries later C. S. Lewis in *The Screwtape Letters* would show why that is the case. Lewis was well aware of the tradition that the demons lived in a constant state of rage and resentment. After all, scholar of Milton that he was, Lewis knew that the great poet invented the word "pandemonium" to describe where the evil ones lived; that word, of course, is now a synonym for raging confusion. In that sense, envy has a certain relationship to wrath. Sadness, of course, was part of the lexicon of the old tradition of the *logismoi*, but sadness is also implicated in *acedia* and is a by-product of gluttony.

It may well be that Gregory, and later Thomas Aquinas, remembered the cautionary story of Saul, the first king of the Jewish people. Despite his military prowess, Saul— who had been formally anointed king—found himself at odds with David, who would become his successor. How it must have tormented Saul when his own son, Jonathan, became David's favored friend, and his own daughter, Michal, became David's wife. First Samuel relates how Saul became increasingly jealous and vengeful, driven by an "evil spirit" (1 Sm 16:14) to the point where he schemed to murder David, after having plotted against him and having driven him into hiding in the desert. Despite their tortured reconciliation, Saul's life ended in suicide (1 Sm 31:4) after failing to win a battle over the Philistines. If there was ever an example of murderous envy, it can be found as a paradigm in the story of King Saul.

In the *Divine Comedy*, Dante likens envy to a kind of blindness. Those who walked on the path up the Mount of Purgatory had their eyes stitched shut to pay for casting an envious eye on others during their lifetime. Thus, to make the punishment fit the crime, the envious had to have their sense of sight and their hearts purged.

Let us consider how this blindness or sadness that Aquinas equated with envy operates within a person. At the success of another, one may harbor an inner sense of grievance, a certain self-pity, resentment, and feeling of superiority. This envy may simply reside within the self, mixed with a smoldering sense of anger, or it may become a goad to action. Let us consider each case in turn.

To internalize envy is rather like internalizing resentment. Only the envious person is aware of the envy. The person envied may go on about life totally oblivious to the fact that he or she is the object of such a powerful negative emotion. The envious one falls into a pattern of constant comparison, adding up real or imagined slights. Interactions with others become self-conscious, suspect, calculated, and full of second-guessing. This brooding only stokes envy further, bringing with it more sourness, unhappiness, and emotional turmoil. Envy easily turns into hatred, and when the person envied makes a gesture of kindness, it only fuels the feeling of envy ("Who does he think he is?" "What does he really mean by saying that?"). In that sense, envy is a kind of anger, and like anger it tends to smolder deep in a person's psyche, touching everything the person sees and feels about another person.

Envy takes a more ominous turn when the perpetrator feels compelled to lash out at the object of his envy as we have seen in the biblical story of Saul. Literature and life are filled with examples, some of them murderous, of those who allow their sense of resentment and envy to spill over into strategies and plots to bring down the other. The textbook example is the scheming Iago, who drives the noble Othello to a tragic end. Hypocritically, Iago warns Othello against the "green-eyed monster" of jealousy, by which Shakespeare obviously meant envy. The phrase "green-eyed" in the Bard's vocabulary meant sickliness, which speaks to how draining and all consuming it can be for a person to be caught up in the cycle of envy. Iago is an evil character, and his evil derives precisely from his envy of Othello and gains more substance by his desire to lash out.

One does not need to consult Shakespeare, however, to find such models of simple jealousy turned to sinful envy. My suspicion is that in every institution—business, university, church, community, or even a family—one can find daily examples of those who thwart the good works or reputation of others by seemingly innocent passivity or through active sabotage. An envious person may bad-mouth a colleague, "accidentally" reveal a secret, or undermine a co-worker by failing to complete his part of a joint project in a timely manner. Contemporary psychological discourse speaks of "passive-aggressive behavior," but lurking beneath that description is envy.

Something else is connected to envy, and it goes by various names. The envious person is inordinately delighted at the bad fortune of others. The Germans call this *Schadenfreude*, while the old moral theology texts called it "morose delectation." To delight in the misfortune of others is an obstacle to kindness and benevolence. For example, in the *Purgatorio*, Dante describes a woman who is so delighted in the downfall of her fellow citizens that she rejoices at the death of her own nephew. Thus the power of envy can marginalize or destroy the capacity for generosity of spirit.

While we separate envy as a distinct vice, it is clear that in life envy is usually bound up with or leads to a whole complex of unhealthy human impulses. Envy is not unconnected to pride—over estimation of one's own worth—and is certainly not free from avarice or anger. The early monks often listed envy as part of a catalog of ills pouring from a disordered life and considered it a failure of Christian humility. These dissatisfactions can be the equivalent of emotional gnats that flit about in our life now and again. But when they are allowed free rein, envy and its allies can become consuming and destructive of one's humanity. The envious person not only poisons his own life, but, given the chance, will allow that poison to seep out and harm others.

Decades ago, the British writer Angus Wilson wrote on envy and made a very perceptive observation. He noted that some of the deadly sins, in their first stage, provided some feeling of satisfaction and pleasure, with lust temporarily sated, or sloth taking its leisure, or gluttony abated after yet another good meal. Envy, however, knows no satisfaction. Wilson perceptively observed: "Envy is crushed with fear, yet never ceasing in its appetite; and it knows no gratification save endless self-torment. It has the ugliness of a trapped rat that has gnawed at its own foot in its effort to escape."[4] Unlike actions of gluttony or lust, in which there may be some initial sensual satisfaction, envy torments from its very inception.

The philosopher Gabriele Taylor pronounces envy as being a particularly nasty vice for at least two reasons. She cites Descartes, who argued that envy tends to generate not only a kind of sadness in the soul but a sadness mingled with hatred, because the envious see someone else possessing a good that the envious person thought was not worthy of them.

Taylor further argues that more sophisticated envy (as opposed to the more immediate pangs of envy toward someone else's good fortune that come almost as a reflex) "can only be felt by those who have self-consciousness, who have an image of themselves and of standing in the world."[5] In other words, anger and pride are never absent to the heart of the envious person. The envious says, in effect, that he or she is of such standing that it hurts to see someone else rewarded or successful.

It is one thing to describe envy, but it is quite another to prescribe antidotes against its presence in our lives. While there may not be a sure, single purgative for envy, the ingredients that would go into such a spiritual medicine would include a more wholesome appreciation of one's own limits and capabilities, the cultivation of a more generous attitude toward others, the discipline of showing gratitude, and a greater sense of proportion about what ultimately matters in life. Those who struggle with envy must also recognize that to resist envy is also to resist illusory pride and smoldering anger. "At its best," Dorothy Sayers once said, "envy is a climber and a snob; at its worst, it is a destroyer—rather than have anybody happier than itself, it will see us all miserable together."[6]

Perhaps the most practical antidote to envy is largeness of heart. Largeness of heart or liberality or generosity is an antidote to both greed and envy. It is common in our religious tradition to say that generous, self-giving love is the highest form of love. To give to the other out of sheer love leaves no room for envy to seethe within us. That is why, in the end, faith and hope will disappear when we are united with God in heaven, but pure love will remain forever.

SIX

SOME PEACEFUL THOUGHTS ON ANGER

> Let everyone be quick to listen, slow to speak, slow to anger;
> your anger does not produce God's righteousness.
>
> JAMES 1:19–20

In 1979, Henry Fairlie wrote a wonderful book based on a series of essays he wrote for the *New Republic* called *The Seven Deadly Sins*. The book was a contemporary look at the ancient list, and the essays in that volume reflected the traditional counting of sins that goes all the way back to Pope Gregory the Great (ca. 540–604) in the sixth century, who named them in the *Moralia in Job* as pride, covetousness, lust, envy, gluttony, anger, and sloth. Gregory, as we noted in the introduction, took the category over from earlier Christian monastic authors who, in fact, listed eight of them. Among the early monks, they were not really understood as "sins" in the technical sense we understand the term today, but as erupting temptations or emotional states or "passions" (the Greeks called them *logismoi*) that clouded the soul, obscuring that "purity of heart," which Jesus said in the Beatitudes allowed one to "see" God.

The seven deadly sins were a standard listing all through the Middle Ages, inspiring artists and writers to depict them vividly in cautionary tales for those who strayed from the straight and narrow. Chaucer's Parson devotes a sermon to them. Dante organizes his Mount of Purgatory with seven terraces, each terrace purging one sin as the souls mount toward heaven. The "seven deadly sins" have even caught the attention of contemporary writers (some of whom we have had occasion to quote in these essays).

What has always struck me as curious, when thinking about this evolution, is how often the early Christian writers, especially the monastic writers, singled out anger as one of the most persistent and dangerous of these sins. St. John Cassian begins discussion of the "demon of anger" by insisting that as long as the demon of anger is within us "we can neither discriminate what is for our good, nor achieve spiritual knowledge nor fulfill our good intentions, nor participate in true life and our intellect will remain impervious to the contemplation of the true divine light." The Sinai ascetic John Climacus thought that anger was a natural fruit of many other sins or temptations, and, in that sense, anger was the offspring of a disordered person. In a famous passage, he has Anger speak of his origins: "I come from many sources and I have more than one father. My mothers are vainglory, avarice, greed. My father is named conceit. My daughters have the names remembrance of wrongs, hate, hostility, and self justification."[7] One of the old Desert Fathers was recorded as saying, "I have spent fourteen years in Scetis asking God night and day to grant me the victory over anger."[8] That is only one saying among nearly twenty of his that have a focus on the sin of anger.

I say that this condemnation of anger is curious because the Bible is filled with stories of anger—and it is not always portrayed as sinful. Moses shattered the tablets of the Law in anger at the sight of the golden calf and the worship of that idol by the Chosen People. The prophets were specialists at anger as they excoriated their people for lack of fidelity to the covenant they made with God at Sinai. Job cries out in anger at the seemingly unjust state of his being. Jesus not only got angry but, as the gospels tell us, lashed out in that anger at the sellers at the Temple, overturning their tables and driving them with whips of cords. The scriptures, not to put too fine a point on it, catalog a good deal of "righteous anger" and stories of angry people, to say nothing of the anger that comes directly from God.

Thus, the question arises: why did those early Christian writers single out anger as a treacherous condition that imperils our humanity and poisons our relationship with God? Perhaps it might be useful at the outset to make a distinction between getting angry and being an angry person. Would it not be a callous person who did not react in anger at the sight of manifest injustice? After all, both the prophets and Jesus got angry at the sight of such manifest injustice and callous indifference to human needs. However, the Bible often described God as "slow to anger" and "rich in mercy."

Are there not things in this world that warrant an angry reaction? Getting angry is different than being an angry person. Everyone, at times, can identify with the character in the movie that opens his window and cries out, "I'm mad as hell and I'm not going to take it anymore!" Such sentiments have driven more than one politician out of office. Perhaps, following a distinction that we find in Latin, we should distinguish indignation (*indignatio*) from anger (*ira*). Thus, there is a difference between indignation and wrath, and this difference will be kept in mind as we explore the sin of anger.

Anyone who pays attention to the media knows how destructive anger (*ira*) can be. We give it different names at times: road rage, eruptions of homicidal anger in the workplace, terrorism in the name of righteous anger against real or perceived injustices, horrendous examples of spousal abuse, and so on. This kind of anger goes beyond reason to take on a life of its own; it boils over. There is a lucrative business in the therapeutic world teaching "anger management" to those whose behavior erupts into, or gives symptoms of, anger that might move into acts of socially unacceptable behavior. Anger in these manifest forms is easy to detect and formidably dangerous when put into practice either by an individual or by what we call the "angry mob."

By and large, the early Christian writers did not always have that kind of anger in mind, since that sort was easy to detect. People know instinctively that when such anger boils over it is destructive and dangerous. What most worried the spiritual writers was internalized anger: the kind fueled by disappointment, wounded pride, real or imagined slights, disappointment with one's situation in life, or other personal affronts that smoldered within a person, often undetectable by others but becoming a lens through which that person saw all of his social life. In our contemporary vocabulary, we often employ specific labels for this kind of anger. We call it "bitterness" or "resentment." In a homily on anger, the fourth-century monk and bishop Basil the Great called it a "sickness of soul, a darkening of thought, an estrangement from God . . . a cause of conflict, a fullness of misfortunes." He ends that catalog, indicating that such a person actually gives birth to a "demon" in his soul. Please note that "demon" did not mean a little creature with horns and a forked tail but a "power" (in Greek *daimon*) that took control of a person. That kind of anger as it wells up in a person leads him or her to become "out of control."

At this point then we can add to what was said earlier. It is one thing to feel and exhibit indignation at some person because of a legitimate grievance. It is quite right to feel such indignation, and we have the prophets as an example of "righteous anger" in the face of manifest injustice or egregious lack of charity. It is quite another thing to be so angry that we become bitter or fully resentful—an angry person.

What ultimately is so bad about internalized anger is this: it hurts only the person who possesses it. Who, after all, is poisoned by one's internal resentment but the one who holds it? One sees that kind of anger in families where a person "doesn't speak to" or "freezes out" another member or members because of issues that, perhaps slight at the time, become magnified into a massive grievance that the person constantly rehearses mentally or externalizes by silence in the face of invitations or other gestures of good will. One sometimes sees a similar kind of angry person in the business environment: the employee or colleague who vents his or her internalized anger with passive-aggressive behavior or through little acts of sabotage or, more sadly, through a depressed life of doing as little as possible in order to "get through the day," enveloped in a fog of barely suppressed unhappiness. The poison of anger is strikingly similar to the poison of envy. In fact, they often show themselves to be two sides of one coin. Such anger may not be as dramatic as eruptions of visible rage, but it is a soul-destroying state of life. It was a commonplace for the ancient writers to describe anger as a smoldering fire whose smoke dimmed every other emotion within a person.

Can such anger be overcome? The great fifth-century monastic writer St. Cassian discusses anger at some length in book eight of the *Institutes*. He states bluntly that the acquisition of peace of mind "must not be made to depend on another's will . . . but it lies rather in our own control." The angry person only exorcises the anger when it dawns on her to stop hurting herself. That observation may seem, at first glance, to be a banality, but upon deeper consideration it is as current and true as anything the most expensive contemporary psychotherapist would say—namely, one must understand why one is angry and, more importantly, learn how to let go of it. Cassian frames the matter in theological terms: the Holy Spirit cannot dwell in company with the spirit of anger. We might put it this way: the price of persistent anger is misery; the reward for letting go of anger is peace of mind.

We might also mention another antidote to persistent anger. The fourth chapter of the *Rule of St. Benedict* has the wonderful title "Tools for Good Works," and here St. Benedict says that the way of the monk should not be the way of the world. Benedict quickly adds: "You are not to act in anger or nurse a grudge." As someone living in community, he knew that a grudge-bearing, angry person was a source of poison for the community. He then, without explanation, adds a few more injunctions: do not be deceitful in your heart; never give a hollow greeting of peace or turn away when someone needs your love. In that almost brusque series of "good works," he might have given us a gem: to avoid anger, turn from the self in love, and care for others. Without saying so, Benedict links anger to self-absorption and pride. He links peace of mind to anger's opposites: love and concern. That strikes me as a wonderful truth even if easy to give and hard to put into play. It works as well in a human family as it does in a monastic community.

Jesus tells us that we must first love God and then our neighbor as ourselves. It is patently the case that the angry soul loves neither neighbor nor self; so to let go of anger is to learn to love oneself and, then, others. If the old monks are correct, and I think they are, it is a hard task to do so but, in the end, worth it for self and neighbor and, ultimately, for the love of God.

SEVEN

SOME HUMBLE THOUGHTS ON PRIDE

Pride goes . . . before a fall.

PROVERBS 16:18

Around the year AD 1124, St. Bernard of Clairvaux (1090–1153) composed a treatise for monks titled *The Steps of Humility and Pride*. His intended monastic audience probably expected an expansion of the famous passage in the *Rule of St. Benedict*, which dealt with the steps of humility. What they got, in fact, was more a treatise on pride, because, as Bernard wrote somewhat whimsically at the end of his tract, he knew more of pride than humility.

Bernard's work is curiously wonderful in the ways in which he sets out the sources (and means of cultivation) of pride. He lists, among other things, the dangers of inordinate curiosity, idle chatter, and senseless foolishness and laughter, trying to be different, considering oneself holier than others, self-justification, minimizing one's sin in confession, and rebellion against authority. Some of these common faults that Bernard found so dangerous seem oddly trivial to the contemporary person. While it is true that "curiosity killed the cat," we prize curiosity as a first step toward creativity and invention. Nor do we always condemn a little foolishness in a person (as in, "I was just fooling around."). Yet to the medieval monastic mind, traits such as curiosity or foolishness were understood in a very specific manner: tendencies exhibited in a person that were self-centered and self-driven in a way that failed to honor human limits. Bernard saw such behavior as signs that the person who indulged in them was calling undue attention to the self. Such desire for attention was, to Bernard's mind, an early symptom of pride—a trait of the "vain glorious" person, who always seeks approval or attention.

What is quite clear in Bernard's writings and the long tradition that comes before him is that pride is always something to be understood in a negative fashion. Pride was regarded with special horror because it was the sin of the rebellious angel of light who became known to us as Lucifer or Satan. It was commonly argued that pride was the fountainhead of all other sin, and the term was usually employed to condemn someone. Warnings about pride, in fact, took on the character of the proverbial. In the seventeenth century, for example, the common charge leveled against the Jansenist nuns of the abbey of Port Royal in

France was that, though they were "pure as angels," they were also "proud as devils."

The English word "pride" is a good old Anglo-Saxon word, and it is not universally used in a pejorative sense. While it is true that the dictionary indicates that the first meaning of the word is taken to mean a "high" (and possibly excessively high) estimation of one's own worth or ability, and secondarily as arrogance or haughtiness, it is also quite rightly used to indicate what is the best in a person, place, or thing. We would not fault someone for advertising a particular cheese as the "pride of Wisconsin," and we certainly hear in my part of the country a lot of talk about "Irish Pride," just as we write songs with lyrics like "I'm proud to be an American." Most recently we have seen the word "pride" used as a title that erases former humiliation. When people use the term "Black Pride," or "Gay Pride," what they mean, in essence, is that, despite their being marginalized or demonized, there is self-worth and value in being black or gay, and their public confession is a source of affirmation—a form of pride.

The more benign understanding of pride in the sense described above is not the kind of pride with which we are concerned. Our interest is to understand the seriousness with which pride is understood in the Catholic tradition as the fountainhead of other sin. Such a consideration might serve as a reminder in a more general sense about how pride can be destructive of humans and of human community.

We might take as our beginning point an observation made by St. Thomas Aquinas in the *Summa Theologiae*. My index to that work indicates nearly thirty places where he discusses pride. In one short discussion, Thomas says that virtue can develop from pride, albeit accidentally. He thought that when a proud person was somehow disabused of pride, the positive character of self-knowledge about one's limitations—that is, humility—comes to the fore.

What Thomas had in mind, I think, was the quality the ancient Greeks called "hubris." Although the Greeks typically understood hubris to be the public performance of shameful behavior simply for the sake of doing it (at least that is what Aristotle took hubris to be), hubris has acquired the added meaning of that overweening self-confidence of someone who acted in a way that brought about his or her destruction, when that one came to a knowledge of some awful truth hitherto hidden. Perhaps there is an allusion in that understanding to the theme found in Proverbs: "Pride goes before a fall." To fall from a position of pride is to recover or discover something of value.

In the kind of pride that manifests itself in unreflective self-confidence and an absolutely certain contentment with one's own intelligence and judgment, we find disaster waiting, as a quick perusal of the daily newspapers attests. This is the kind of pride that some writers have called "arrogant pride." How often do we read of political figures so confident in their own judgment that cautionary warnings are looked upon as "going soft"? How many corporate heads are so enamored of their own genius that telltale warning signs are ignored or salutary advice is deemed unworthy of a hearing? Even worse are those instances where individuals, pumped up with indications of their infallibility, not only resist caution, but mock those who offer it. To inherent pride they add ungodly pleasure in the misfortune accruing to those who are perceived as suckers or dimwits and who do not enjoy the wit and cleverness of the self-confident person. This kind of pride manifests itself as arrogance, and when the arrogant stumble, we take some unseemly delight in watching them fall. In fact, such satisfaction (not always a virtue!) comes because there are clusters of repellent manifestations of human pride like arrogance hovering around overweening pride—conceit and vanity come immediately to mind. There is also that sense of satisfaction in the persons who are brought low because they considered themselves too bright to be caught. Pride, the Bible says, goes before a fall.

How did the Christian tradition come to regard pride so negatively? Why has Lucifer—the angelic Bearer of Light—become the paradigmatic figure of pride? Surely, part of the answer is to be found in the fact that the proud person is totally committed to the self, or, to say it another way, the proud person stands outside the community of others, totally reliant on the self. Such total autonomy, of course, admits no reliance on or communion with another (hence, love is bracketed from one's experience) and, in its extreme form, cannot allow for the "fear of the Lord," which the scriptures describe as the beginning of wisdom. That total confidence in the self is caught perfectly in Lucifer's cry of *non serviam!*—"I will not serve!"

Dante caught the character of demonic pride perfectly. Satan is sunk in an icy lake bootlessly flapping his wings to escape his arctic trap. He is depicted as a drooling, inarticulate beast. He is in ice because he is at the farthest point from the warming love of God, and he is a mumbling monster because he has lost his angelic intelligence. Dante's Satan is the perfect example of pride brought low.

There is an ancient but powerful shorthand description of sinfulness in Christian theology that is often attributed to Martin Luther: *incurvatus in se*—turned in upon the self. We have had occasions to mention that condition before in these pages. It is also a perfect description of pride. A spirit of unreflective self-sufficiency turns a person into an impregnable bastion of self-love that admits of no entrance to another, much less to God. Dorothy Sayers caught the essence of this kind of pride by noting how it goes under many names in modern society: "It is the sin which proclaims that Man can produce out of his own wits, and his own impulses and his own imagination the standards, by which he lives. . . . The name which Pride walks the world at this moment is the Perfectibility of Man or the doctrine of Progress and its specialty is the making of blueprints for Utopia and the establishing the Kingdom of Man on earth."[9]

The opposite of pride is humility. In no sense is humility to be taken as that kind of faux modesty that one sees in some self-loving athlete or actor who pretends that he is not God's gift to humanity but really believes that he is. That kind of faux depreciation is a staple item of acceptance speeches at the annual Academy Awards show or the "ah shucks" kind of self-deprecating speech we hear from politicians on the stump. We all have a nose for insincerity, and almost inevitably we find it to have a bad odor.

Humility is the most attractive of virtues. To be humble is to understand that one is not totally self-sufficient, that one depends on the encouragement of others and on their love, that one is free enough to ask for the help and counsel of others, that one is able to be grateful. Indeed, the most wonderful offspring of humility is gratitude—the capacity to thank someone or to thank many. Not to be able to be grateful is an apt description of the one who is proud. Put simply, the proud person is an ingrate. By contrast, the authentically humble person is most attractive. It is good to remember that the root meaning of humility comes from the Latin word for the earth (*humus*). The humble person is an "earthy" person and is to be carefully distinguished from the *humiliated* person—someone who is driven into the ground. The proud person, by contrast, sees nothing beyond his own self. As seen earlier, Jesus tells a story about a rich person who, happy about the abundance of his crops, tears down his barns to build bigger ones. When these new barns are filled and ample goods laid up for many years, he says to himself, "Take your ease, eat, drink, and be merry" (Lk 12:16–20).

Rebecca DeYoung relates a wonderful story about the relationship of pride to an honest confession of humility. The popular radio host and entertainer Garrison Keillor once confessed in an interview that he "was desperate to win all the little merit badges and trinkets of my profession and I am of less real use in this world than any good cleaning lady."[10]

The British Dominican Timothy Radcliffe, in a wonderful little book titled *What is the Point of Being a Christian?*, notes that in Luke's parable of the rich man and his granaries, the pronoun "I" is used eleven times, while God's response begins with the simple harsh word "fool." God breaks in to shatter the narcissistic prison walls of the rich man's "stupid self-centeredness," telling him that this very night his soul will be demanded of him. Radcliffe uses that gospel parable to illustrate a point about how, for a Christian, there must be a way of shifting from "I" to "we." To be imprisoned in the "I" is to be numbered among the proud; to be able to say "we" is to be fully human.

It is important, however, to observe a cautionary note at this point. In one of the most famous passages in the scriptures, Jesus, echoing the command in Deuteronomy 6:5, says that we are to love God with our heart, mind, and soul. Jesus then adds that we should love our neighbor as *ourselves*. To put it differently, Jesus demands that we love God, neighbor, and self. There is no merit in self-hate. There is an unfortunate fact that the world around us is made up of people who take enormous pleasure in denigrating others—either individually (think of the bully), or as a class or race. The person who is the subject of denigration often ends up with a crushed sense of self-worth. A person is thus described as a self-hater or one suffering from what is called "low self-esteem."

In that sense, the polar opposite of overweening pride is self-hatred. Humility becomes humiliation. To hate oneself is a parody of what Jesus insists is the norm, namely, to hold up everyone (including myself) as a child of God, made in the divine image and likeness, who is of radical worth. There is a reason why Jesus frequently held up the least esteemed—the leper, the tax collector, the prostitute, etc.—for special recognition and love. Indeed, one could make the case that everyone "from the moment of conception to natural death" (to borrow the language of the pro-life movement, and, indeed, the whole social doctrine of the Church is based on the proposition) is loved by God and lovable as God's creature. The conclusion of those truths is simply this: to grind down the other, to spurn the other singly or as a group, is to exalt the self in a way that falls naturally under the penumbra of wicked pride by exalting oneself at the expense of the other.

There is a very fine line to be drawn between self-denial and self-hatred. We are asked by Jesus to "deny oneself," but that does not mean that we should demean ourselves to the extent that we put ourselves under the penumbra of despair. The cultivated Christian life demands a kind of "triangulation" by which we love self and others in relationship to our love of God. This demand is not, by and large, something that happens in an instant. It is the product of a long path of following the One who is the Way.

EPILOGUE:
PURITY OF HEART

Careful readers of this book will notice how frequently citations have come from St. Matthew's gospel in general and chapters 5–7 in particular. This was no accident. Those chapters articulate what is more generally known as the "Sermon on the Mount." It is commonplace in biblical commentary to note that Matthew had as a template for those chapters the revelation of the *Torah* received by Moses on Mount Sinai. In that sense, at least, the material in Matthew 5–7 can be seen as a new *Torah* in which Jesus, based without question on the Mosaic Law, expands, perfects, and articulates anew God's revelation to his people. Jesus himself makes this clear as part of this section: "Do not think that I have come to abolish the law or the prophets. I have come not to abolish but to fulfill" (Mt 5:17). What a fulfillment it is as Jesus amplifies the laws about anger, adultery, divorce, oaths, and the law of retaliation until, as a climax, he proclaims: "Love your enemies, pray for those who persecute you, so that you may be children of your Father in heaven . . . " (Mt 5:44). Subsequent teachings deal with the fundamental ascetic practices of prayer, fasting, and almsgiving, followed by a series of images, metaphors, and exhortations demanding that what we appear to be outwardly must conform to what we are in the heart. The sermon ends with Jesus using another metaphor to argue that it is only by internalizing what he teaches that his follower be secure: "Everyone who hears these words and acts upon them will be like a wise man who builds his house on rock . . ." (Mt 7:24).

It is no wonder, then, that when we begin to think about how we might attain purity of heart, we go back to that place in the gospel where Jesus talks about purity of heart, namely, in the Sermon on the Mount where Jesus teaches the Beatitudes. We began by recalling that the early monastic writers saw the eight *logismoi* or passions and later the seven deadly sins as obstacles to attaining that purity of heart that Jesus, in the Beatitudes, declared as a necessary condition for seeing God: "Blessed are the clean of heart, for they shall see God" (Mt 5:8). The sentiment expressed by Jesus was not peculiar to him. He was a pious Jew and, as such, knew that the same sentiment, in a somewhat different form, was expressed by the psalmist:

> Who shall ascend the hill of
> the Lord

> And who shall stand in his
> holy place?
> Those who have clean hands
> and pure hearts. (Ps 24:3–4)

The key word in that short passage is "heart." The Bible uses the word "heart" over a thousand times. It almost never means the physical organ of a person; it stands as a shorthand term to describe the innermost place of a human being. The *Catechism of the Catholic Church* describes the biblical understanding of the heart well, as "our hidden center, beyond the grasp of our reason and of others; only the Spirit of God can fathom the human heart and know it fully. The heart is the place of truth, where we choose life or death. It is the place of encounter, because as image of God we live in relation: it is the place of covenant" (*CCC*, 2563).

When we begin to notice the word "heart" in the scriptures, we will often see it as described in polar terms. The scriptures speak of the warmed heart and the hardened heart, of the secrets of the heart for both good and evil, as the place from which comes forth both our link to God and our sinfulness. Here are twin examples of this polarity from the words of Jesus. In one place, he sees the heart as the place of sin: "But what comes out of the mouth proceeds from the heart and that is what defiles. For out of the heart comes evil intentions, murder, adultery, fornication, theft, false witness, slander. These are what defile a person . . . " (Mt 15:18–20).

By contrast, Jesus invites his hearers to follow him using as an example his own heart: "Come to me all of you who are weary and are carrying heavy burdens and I will give you rest. Take my yoke upon you and learn from me; for I am gentle and humble of heart and you will find rest for your souls. For my yoke is easy and my burden is light" (Mt 11:28–30).

The seven deadly sins, then, obstruct the pure heart, and it is the pure heart that "sees God." In order to "see God" one must be able to "see" outside the self to the other. The one thing that is constant in our analysis of the sins we have discussed is that every one of them, each in its own way, implicates the primacy and the perceived sufficiency of the self. Pride is about the personal standing and glory of *me* over the others; envy is about *me* in relation to another; gluttony and lust and greed satisfy *my* needs, desires, and impulses; sloth gives *me* respite; anger lashes out from *my* sense of hurt; etc. This exaltation of the self is at a cost to our relationship to the other and to God.

It would be an error to think that we must obliterate or denigrate the self in order to love neighbor and God. This is a common misunderstanding of the virtue of humility. Christianity is not about the erasure of the self, but it is very much about how we understand ourselves in relationship to others and to God. Christian humility implies, of necessity, relationship. The person who hates human company or who is incapable of loving another person is not the model of humility. Humility is the virtue by which we grasp that there is an order in the way we relate to ourselves and to others.

Furthermore, we can understand the pure heart both in terms of our human way of living and the human way of living in relationship to grace. The ancients praised the virtue of *prudence*, that habit by which we avoided extremes of behavior. The prudent person is one who did not choose to be prodigal with human goods nor avaricious, but was sensible in husbanding the possessions he or she had. Prudence is the judgment by which we follow the golden mean of avoiding extremes at both ends: the person of courage avoids both foolhardiness on one hand and excessive timidity on the other. The other traditional cardinal virtues of justice, fortitude, and temperance showed themselves as virtuous in that they manifested prudence. Prudence is a medium; fortitude is the medium between foolhardiness and timidity just as temperance is the middle way between excess and parsimony.

It is clear in our analysis of the seven deadly sins that the Catholic commentators (especially St. Thomas Aquinas) drew on the ancients, especially Aristotle's *Ethics*, for their analysis of the virtues opposing the deadly sins. However, they were also conscious of the so-called theological virtues (so named because their object is God) of faith, hope, and charity. These virtues find their final fulfillment in the embrace of God, as St. Paul famously put it: "Now I know only in part: then I will know fully even as I have been fully known. And now faith, hope and love abide; these three; but the greatest of these is love" (1 Cor 13:12b–13).

To summarize the matter, those who desire purity of heart seek, under the impulse of grace, to do two things that are complementary but different in degree: first, to live lives that—morally speaking—follow the middle way by the exercise of prudence; second, to follow that way of living with faith, hoping for the "not yet" before us, and exercising that love that St. Paul describes as the greatest virtue of all.

We can then ask, how do the theological virtues correlate with purity of heart? We can begin to answer that question with a focus on love. Love, in the theological sense, derives from the Gospel imperative that there is no greater love than the willingness to give all for the sake of the other: "This is my commandment: that you love one another as I have loved you. No one has greater love than this, to lay down one's life for one's friends" (Jn 15:12). Love, then, is going outside the self—even to the point of giving one's own life.

That great saying of Jesus, one of the most famous in John's gospel, has within it the model of Jesus himself, since he himself, in fact, did give up his life for the sake of others. The love of which Jesus speaks is not merely a moral dictum but a performative observation in which Jesus says, in effect, that his demonstration of love is precisely this: I will show you what love is by giving myself up on the Cross. The apex of life, in short, is my willingness to love you at the greatest risk to myself.

This demand of the Cross may be read as an impossible ideal, and it is true that most of us are not called upon to make enormous sacrifices like those of the martyrs either ancient or contemporary; rare is the person who must go to the cross in any literal sense of the term. All of us, however, face our own challenges, and, likewise, all of us are blessed to the degree that we strive for purity of heart. The issue is: how do we do that in practice? There is no easy, "one fits all" answer to that question. That being said, it is also the case that we can draw from the ancient tradition of Christian spirituality to make some useful generalizations. From the almost infinite number of models, examples, maxims, and disciplines in that tradition, I have culled out seven "practices" so as to create a wobbly sort of symmetry with the number "seven" we have used with such frequency in describing sin.

SEVEN BEST PRACTICES

First, if it is the case that one or many of the deadly sins is gripping someone, the person should take the primary step of remembering God to equip himself or herself to escape the clutches of sin. This may sound rather obvious, but the "remembrance of God" is a very old theme in the writings of the early Fathers of the Church. To remember God is to forget, for a moment, one's own self in order to recognize the reality of God, who is "closer to us than we are to ourselves," as St. Augustine once beautifully said.

To remember God does not mean that we should (or even could) live in some sort of permanent mystic trance. Rather, it means that in our everyday lives we can reflect that we are in the presence of God. Concrete gestures like starting the day with the Sign of the Cross, or pausing to say a word of thanksgiving as we eat, or marking the week by attendance at liturgy is to insert awareness of God's presence. The Bible sometimes calls this the "fear of the Lord," which is described in the book of Proverbs as the beginning of wisdom. "Fear of the Lord" does not mean some kind of terror-filled existence (a belief that we are constantly under divine wrath), but it does mean that we are sensitive to the fact that we are not the be-all or end-all of existence. We are not totally independent, alone, or the sole reason of our existence. Rather, we are in relationship to the ultimate meaning of existence, which is God.

Second, along with remembering God in our daily lives, we must—by fits and starts if necessary—cultivate the habit of generosity. When speaking of generosity, we should not automatically think of the lavish giving of goods or things. The etymological root of generosity comes from the word *genus* meaning highborn or the class of nobility. It came to mean the noble act of concern or of giving out of one's abundance. Generosity begins with awareness of others. The generous person begins with a sense of those who are closest to them: spouses to each other; parents to children; individuals to families, neighbors, coworkers, etc. It is quite easy to pray for one's enemies in the abstract, but quite difficult to be generous to an ungrateful family member or an irritating neighbor. Jesus has a quite wonderful saying in this regard: "For if you love those who love you, what reward do you have? Do not even the tax collectors do the same? And if you greet only your brothers and sisters, what more are you doing than others? Do not even the gentiles do the same?" (Mt 5:46–47).

It is quite clear that generosity is an antidote to many, if not most, of the sinful impulses that have been the subject of this book. The envious, wrathful, proud, etc., are so constricted by their own needs and desires that they are incapable of generosity. Of course, it is clear that the kind of generosity of which we are speaking is a muted form of self-giving love or at least an impulse that leads to love, and authentic love is a deadly foe to sin. True love gives, while lust and gluttony take. It is the kind of love that one sees in the care of a parent for a child, of one spouse for another, in the generosity one shows for a needy neighbor. Such love is not necessarily dramatic; it often manifests itself in those small gestures of care and concern that, when seen, move us.

Such gestures of generosity and concern are forms of love that stand in sharp contrast to acts of pettiness, selfishness, and heedless indifference or cruelty. They are the acts that, in the words of the great saints and mystics, "mend the world." They are the kinds of acts that expand; the more one loves in closeness, the more one is inclined to expand that love to others.

To be a generous person is to be for others. The anti-Nazi martyr Dietrich Bonhoeffer once described Jesus as "the man for others." To be a generous person is to be one who shares, whether that sharing involves words or time or concern or goods or whatever.

Third, and not unconnected to the first two, the person who desires purity of heart must be a person who both forgives and petitions for forgiveness. To forgive, of course, is an exercise of generosity. At times, it is true, it is extremely difficult to forgive someone who has wounded us in some fashion. When St. Augustine preached on the Lord's Prayer, he would not infrequently chide his congregation, saying that when they recited that prayer together late in the liturgy they would be hypocrites if they asked for forgiveness when there were some in the congregation that, in their hearts, they had not forgiven. Augustine well understood that it was hard (humanly) to let go of grievances. However, as we have already noted, harboring grievances in our minds and hearts enhances both a smoldering spirit of wrath and, more to the point, a kind of spiritual poison that affects everything we do. Not to forgive is a restriction of generosity and, by extension, our capacity to love.

To forgive is only half the matter, however. The other side of this issue is to ask for forgiveness. To request to be forgiven brings forth any number of advantages. In the first place we ask for forgiveness so as to repair hurts and disaffections that we have caused. Doing so repairs not just our relationship with one other person but the dissensions and alienations that can affect an entire community: "If you remember that your brother or sister has something against you, leave your gift before the altar and go; first be reconciled to your brother and sister and then come and offer your gift" (Mt 5:23–24). Of course, to ask for forgiveness demands something that we all find hard to do: to admit we are wrong and seek amends for that wrong.

Reconciliation is not only a matter of one-to-one issues. There is also the temptation to be alienated from others by reason of deep-seated prejudice. We are at odds with others, sometimes in the most general or abstract way, because we do not like their race, their religion, their habits, their opinions, or their other "otherness." We shun such people or judge them *a priori* or talk down about them or, God forbid, even lash out at them. It is not a matter of "having an opinion" but a spirit of disdain that easily grows into verbal violence and, not infrequently, into real violence. Jesus sets the example here by being willing, to borrow an older book title, to "be in bad company." Jesus did not despise the tax collector or the prostitute; he held up the Samaritan as a model; he spoke to the shunned woman at the well; he severely criticized the religious and social elite; and, according to Luke, one of his last loving conversational exchanges was with a condemned prisoner.

Reconciliation, finally, is also a sacrament. It is the sign that we are reconciled with the Christian community and, of course, God. The *Catechism of the Catholic Church* catches this fact succinctly: "Sin is before else an offense against God, a rupture of communion with him. At the same time it damages communion with the church. For this reason conversion entails both God's forgiveness and reconciliation with the church, which are expressed and accomplished liturgically by the sacrament of Penance and Reconciliation" (*CCC*, 1440).

In the fourth place, we should learn to cultivate the ascetic practices recommended by Jesus in his Sermon on the Mount as recorded in Matthew 5–7. Those practices of prayer, fasting, and almsgiving were a kind of framework for leading the kind of life that Jesus saw as a righteous one. The history of Christianity indicates that there were many different ways in which these practices were carried out. We will take up each in turn with a few suggestions about how the practices may be applied to the ordinary life of the Christian.

Jesus recommends prayer—which we will describe here using the classical formulation of St. John of Damascus—as turning the heart and mind to God. Without specifying the many diverse forms of prayer (private and communal, verbal and meditative, etc.), we will link this discipline with the observations made in the first of these "best practices," that to have a pure heart we must cultivate the habit of remembering God. The word "habit" is used advisedly because prayer ought not to be restricted to those momentary occasions when we articulate only something for our own benefit ("Lord, let me pass the calculus exam," or "Dear God, let me win the lottery"). Rather, prayer must be the deep sense that we depend on God for our very existence, our well-being, our needs, our wounds, and our final destiny. The habit of remembering God means simply that on a regular basis we articulate that relationship to God in some explicit manner. To have the habit of prayer is to be in relation; it is the most secure guard against the soul-destroying situation of being only for one's own self. Of course, we can pray on our own, but it is also an essential fact that our prayer ought to be communal, since, as Jesus taught, "Where two or three are gathered together, there I am in the midst of you" (Mt 18:20). As the Church teaches,

Christ is present in the worship community, speaking to us through Word and Eucharist.

We have used the word "habit" in relation to prayer. What is meant by this term is that the person who desires purity of heart ought to turn the heart and mind to God as part of the texture of his or her life. That habit might be as simple as "remembering God," at the start and close of each day or before meals, or more formally in participation in the liturgical life of the Church. The crucial point is to have some "place" for God in our ordinary lives.

Jesus also preached the ascetic practice of fasting. As a pious Jew, he of course fasted as part of his religious practice and, famously, initiated his public life fasting in the desert. Fasting is a perfect example of an ascetic practice because it asks that we do something onerous—reducing food and drink—not as an absolute good in itself but in order to attain something more intensely spiritual: focus of the mind and heart, solidarity with those who hunger, deprivation in order to make us more mindful, etc.

Fasting is not an end in itself. Every ascetic practice is a means to an end. The word "asceticism" itself derives from athletic training. The athlete practices not for the sake of practice but for a larger goal, just as a religious person "fasts" for a purpose. Those who fast as an end in itself are not being religious; they are likely suffering from an eating disorder.

However, fasting and its cousin, abstinence, do not only mean control of nourishment. To fast or abstain may also have as its target other forms of self-satisfaction that have a tendency to control us. There are many forms of "abstinence" that can serve us in our desire to attain a pure heart. Suppose, for example, we know that we require in our contemporary lives more attention to quiet and reflection. To fill that need, "giving up" desserts or late-night snacks will likely not prove terribly useful. However, there are many examples of "abstinence" that many of us might find more difficult but, at the same time, more profitable: turning off the television on a given day, for example; shutting down the computer for half the day; silencing the iPhone; working without the constant sound of the radio; resisting the urge to listen to so much peripheral "news" or music on the car radio.

The benefits of such "electronic fasting" could be many. One would be to reawaken us to how much time in our life we waste on frivolous activities. Another might be to heal our imaginations against the propaganda, semi-pornography, meretricious manipulations of urging us to consume more or buy more, etc.

There are other modes of "fasting" that we could imagine as beneficial as we attempt to center our hearts. One mode might be to ask ourselves a very simple question: how much time do we waste, and to what end? Being more conscious about how we spend time mindlessly is to resist that kind of idleness (which is, as the cliché has it, "the devil's workshop") that pampers the self at the expense of others to whom we owe a duty, like those in our family or those who would benefit from our supportive friendship. Another mode can also be framed in the form of a question: do we adequately distinguish what we need from what we want? All of us who are blessed with some material comfort would do well to fast from superfluous spending on things we do not need but simply want. If we could be a bit more imaginative about how we understand the ascetic practice of fasting or abstinence, we will be able to cultivate a more centered and disciplined life by which we put to good use the good things God has given us for creature comfort.

Jesus tells us in the Beatitudes that the other great ascetic practice is almsgiving, which we might call today "generosity to the other in need." Almsgiving is a free act of giving, beyond that which we owe others out of justice. When we hear the word "almsgiving" we tend to think of donations given to the poor, and it is the case that from its beginnings the Christian community has emphasized sustenance to the poor both at the communal and individual level. As the Church emerged from the period of persecution, it began a program to underwrite hospices, hospitals, schools, orphanages, etc., in a tradition that comes down to the present.

Individuals have also felt it part of their normal religious practice to give generously to those who are in need. That is why we emphasize the so-called seven "corporal works of mercy" as part of our normal religious instruction. To do this both at a communal and individual level is not some kind of weak "social Christianity" but, as Pope Benedict wrote in *God is Love*, one of the three pillars of Christianity (the others being worship, and evangelization or witness).

Almsgiving, broadly understood, is on first inspection a powerful antidote to the selfishness underlying the seven deadly sins. It is a practice that blunts avarice, obviously, but it is also an exercise that leads us to "forget the self" out of love, and doing that is sure remedy of other sinful dispositions.

There is also another way of understanding almsgiving that goes beyond generosity with our material goods. We can also give others things that are "ours." We can be generously giving, to cite one example, of our time. In giving time—to members of our families, our friends, neighbors, those who are extended members of our community—we go out from the self to serve others. Every parish bulletin cries out for us to donate time in the food and clothing pantry, to teach CCD classes, to serve at times of funerals, etc. When we volunteer, we are giving the alms of our time. We can also give our expertise in order to help teach the ignorant, to instruct the immigrant in our language, to hold and nurture babies, and to care for underinstructed children.

To give alms—broadly construed—is a fundamental way of demonstrating by action that our religious life has not been narrowed down to some kind of individualistic connection between "me and God." It is also a way of demonstrating the truth of the doctrine of the Mystical Body of Christ. When St. Paul uses that image, he is careful to point out that when we think of the human body, we know by instinct that all parts are dependent on each other, so that when there is a pain or illness in one part, it is the person that is ailing. Paul says, "The eye cannot say to the hand, 'I have no need of you'" (1 Cor 12:21). At the conclusion of that long passage, Paul concludes, "Now you are the body of Christ and individually members of it" (12:27). The fundamental point is that in almsgiving (and in many other ways) we give recognition to the intimate connection between one person and another and to that connection being construed as belonging "to Christ."

Fifth and finally, to seek purity of heart is to take responsibility for the profound gift of grace given to us by our Baptism—which makes us children of God and members of the communion of fellow believers called the People of God. This membership is pure grace, and that means we did not earn it or deserve it; it comes purely as a gift from God. It is the ungrateful person, however, who is indifferent to a gift or misuses it. Every gift comes with some kind of responsibility. Of course, nobody expects the ordinary Catholic to take that responsibility so seriously that family is neglected or duties of life left unperformed—that one become, as it were, a contemplative monk if one were not called to that state. St. Francis de Sales wrote in the opening pages of his brilliant book *Introduction to the Devout Life* that the devotion of the married woman was not that of the nun, just as the local bishop would be wrong to live like a Carthusian hermit.

If we as ordinary people "in the pew" desire to cultivate purity of heart, we need to seamlessly integrate, to the degree appropriate, the sacramental life of the Church into daily life as an effortless disposition, from the *sine qua non* of participation in the liturgy to the observance of those moments when other sacramental occasions arrive. In a way, we can think of our ordinary Christian life as the matrix out of which we are formed as fully human. To be fully human, in the Christian view of things, is to strive for purity of heart. Of course, we are humans and not angels, so the tug of the flesh—the desire to eat more, to allow a lustful glance, to become irate at an annoying person—is a constant in our lives. The supreme realist, St. Paul, put it bluntly: "All have sinned and fallen short of the glory of God; they are now justified by his grace as a gift through the redemption that is in Christ Jesus" (Rom 3:23–24).

The only unforgivable sin is the one for which we do not seek forgiveness. *Every* week we confess our sins as we begin the liturgy. Spiritual masters ask us to ask forgiveness as part of our night prayers. We have open to us the sacrament of Reconciliation. We hope for the last rites as we come to an end of our lives. To put it in a few words: only God is holy; the best we can hope for is that his gift (which is grace) is to give us some share in that holiness. Again, let St. Paul provide us with the consoling words: "Where sin increased, grace abounded all the more so that just as sin abounded in death, so grace might also exercise dominion through justification, leading us to eternal life through Jesus Christ Our Lord" (Rom 5:20–21).

We should also note that gratitude, finally, is an absolutely foundational platform for cultivating the habit of prayer. After all, "eucharist," one of the most precious words in the Christian vocabulary, comes from the Greek verb meaning "to give thanks." If we are grateful persons, we know that what comes to us (including life itself!) is gift, and for those gifts, and many others like them, we owe thanks. Even the prayer of petition is an implicit acknowledgment that more gifts can come—just as every prayer asking forgiveness reflects an awareness that we can be forgiven.

CONCLUSION

This book has been about sin. Seven of them, in fact. Sin is part of the human condition, but need not be the chief characteristic of what it means to be human.

The medieval theologians contrasted the seven deadly sins with the seven gifts of the Holy Spirit drawn from a passage in Isaiah 11: wisdom, understanding, counsel, fortitude, knowledge, piety, and fear of the Lord (*CCC*, 1831 and 1845). In fact, those same medieval thinkers searched the tradition for other sets of seven like the petitions of the Lord's Prayer, the seven utterances of Jesus on the Cross, the seven Beatitudes, etc., to act as a counterbalance to the "deadly" effects of sin. One can think of these various strategies as "remedies"—healing instruments to counteract our tendency to sin.

In the final analysis, it might be said that all those strategies and others like them were an attempt to encourage people to live simple, Christian lives. To live as a Christian is to be a spiritual person and not a fleshly one. That distinction comes from St. Paul who, famously, in Romans 8, contrasts life in the Spirit and life in the flesh. To live in the flesh is to be "hostile to God" (8:8), but to live in the Spirit gives us the "spirit of adoption by which we cry out Abba! Father!" (8:15). Paul is not contrasting body and spirit (we all live as embodied persons) but body and flesh.

The person, according to Paul, who is truly spiritual is one who possesses what he calls the "Spirit of Christ": that living power by which we become fully human, loving ourselves as bearing the image of God, loving others because they bear that same image, and loving God who is the source of all. In fact, we know that those who live only for the "flesh" lack a certain beauty. In the final analysis, we instinctively recoil from the haughty, the self-indulgent, the bitter, or the lascivious persons—even when those persons are ourselves. We would prefer to live temperate lives with a capacity for friendship and love. We know, almost by instinct, that a life of sin (i.e., a life of the flesh) is repugnant upon examination. We also know, almost by instinct, that being a giving person nourishes us by a seeming paradox: to the degree that we reach out to others, we also nourish ourselves before the face of God. In that sense, we are free persons who rightly use the goods of this world without being bound by them.

It is common today to bandy about the word "spirituality" to cover any kind of desire to have an "experience" (like yoga or running or eating healthily, etc.), but the proper meaning of spirituality is to live according to the framework set out by St. Paul in Romans 8: to live a life under the impulse of the Holy Spirit and not allow ourselves to be sunk into the mire of "everydayness" without any sense of our destiny. It is to live in virtue (the word means

"strength") and not in vice (which means "weakness") after the example given to us by Jesus Christ in the power of
the Spirit.

In other words, according to Paul, the spiritual life finds
its foundation in living in the Spirit and not in the flesh
(see Rom 8:9). By flesh, Paul does not mean the body but
those impulses by which we are prey to death, whereas
those who live in the Spirit are oriented towards eternal
life through the promise of Christ's own resurrection. Paul
ends his discussion of life in the Spirit with these memorable words: "When we cry 'Abba! Father!' it is that very
Spirit bearing witness with our spirit that we are children
of God, then heirs of God and joint heirs of Christ . . ."
(Rom 8:15b–17).

With specific reference to the seven sins we have been
discussing in this book, we can learn something from
the discussion of St. Thomas Aquinas in the *Summa* (II.
II, 34.5). Thomas calls these sins "capital sins" noting
that the word "capital" comes from the Latin word *caput*,
meaning "the head." They are called "capital sins," by
the use of a metaphor: they are the "head" or the source
of other sins. They "poison the well" of the moral life.
In Thomas's understanding of the matter, a sin like envy
or gluttony is not just psychological weakness but true
vice. These sins spring from choices that in themselves
are wrong but, in addition, as we have noted, spawn other

vices as from a source. In that sense, they are less to be understood as acts and more as dispositions that trigger other vices. Often, as Thomas will say in discussing a particular capital sin, they can lead, if not amended, to despair.

We can see the truth of what Thomas is saying if we think of some basic sin and give it a contemporary name. Racism will suffice as an example. If a person allows himself or herself to cultivate hatred or even an intense dislike for a certain race (Chinese, African-American, Semitic—pick a race) simply on the basis of race, it is easy to see how, on the basis of that dislike, that person can be indifferent to the plight of another. He can even act with prejudice toward that person or group or exalt his own racial profile at the expense of that person, either personally or as an abstract object of his prejudice. One can, upon reflection, name the sentiments of the heart that spring from that prejudice: pride, wrath, etc.

The root evil of racism is that it reduces individuals to an abstraction. We dislike this or that race without reference to this or that person. It condemns before it knows. It refuses human encounter in the name of some ethnic category. Racism tends to resist knowing a person before the fact and in the process condemns whole classes out of some kind of judgment that neglects the reality of a person.

Jesus says that where your treasure is there is also your heart (Mt 6:21). It is a brilliant observation, for it means quite simply that your deepest desire frames and colors who you are. It is for that reason that we come back again to the heart. If, as we have insisted, the heart stands for the true center of who we are, then it is our heart that we must keep open to God's grace and where we must be most true and open about who we are and to what we must aspire. It is the heart that tells finally who we are.

When the Lenten season rolls around each year, we hear the prophet Joel calling for repentance. There is a particular line in that passage read at the liturgy that has always struck me powerfully. Joel cries out: "Rend your hearts, not your garments" (Jl 2:13). It was the Jewish custom to show remorse, sadness, and especially mourning at the time of a funeral by tearing at one's clothing. Joel says, however, it is our hearts that must be rent, because it is in the heart where our deepest meaning rests.

It is a radical truth of Christianity that none of us is perfect; we constantly need to repent and be converted. Everyone knows this to be the case (unless we are fully in the grip of pride!), and the Church knows it also, because it invites us to consider our sins at the beginning of every liturgy. Conversion simply means to start anew. At its root, conversion means turning toward God in a fresh way. In every conversion there is also an aversion. When we turn toward, we turn away from. That is the way to understand our purification of the heart: every turn toward God has within it a turning away from that which is not God.

Catholics have an old practice known as "the examination of conscience." We are encouraged to scrutinize ourselves (let conscience stand for heart!) both before we go the sacrament of Reconciliation and, as a pious practice, on a daily basis before we retire. However, it is a practice that we can also use as the occasion arises, for example, when we enter the Lenten season or when we feel some sense of remorse (the word "remorse" means to "bite again") for something we have done or when we are at a time when we want a fresh start. Such an examination done in our own interiority is like the old Southern expression of "getting my heart right."

Finally, we must not link the search to amend our hearts in any solipsistic manner. There is nothing individualistic about the cultivation of the pure heart, even though "heart" stands for what is deepest and most true about ourselves. We are, after all, social beings. All of the deadly sins can be understood as having a relationship to others: the glutton ignores the needs of others, the lustful seeks to use another, the person of pride disdain, those who are seen to be below him, etc. Sacred scripture puts it bluntly: "Those who say 'I love God' and hate their brothers or sisters are liars; for those who do not love their brothers or sisters whom they have seen cannot love

God whom they have not seen. The commandment we have from him is this: those who love God must love their brothers and sisters also" (1 Jn 4:20–21).

NOTES

1. Gabriele Taylor, *Deadly Vices* (Oxford: Clarendon, 2006), 1.

2. Henry Fairlie, *The Seven Deadly Sins Today* (Notre Dame, IN: University of Notre Dame Press, 1979), 178.

3. Robert C. Solomon, *Wicked Pleasures: Meditations on the Seven "Deadly" Sins* (Rowman & Littlefield, 2000), 87.

4. W. H. Auden, Cyril Connolly, Angus Wilson, Patrick Leigh Fermor, Christopher Sykes, Evelyn Waugh, *The Seven Deadly Sins* (New York: Morrow, 1962), 11.

5. *Deadly Vices*, 46.

6. Dorothy Sayers, *The Other Six Deadly Sins* (London: Methuen, 1941), 20.

7. *The Ladder of Monks*, Step #8.

8. Benedicta Ward, *The Sayings of the Desert Fathers* (Kalamazoo: Cistercian Publications, 1975), 22.

9. *The Other Six Deadly Sins*, 26.

10. Rebecca Konyndyk DeYoung, *Glittering Vices* (Grand Rapids, MI: Brazos, 2009), 59.

FOR FURTHER READING

On the monastic origin and development of the eight passions the standard treatise is Evagrius Ponticus's *Prak-
tikos: Chapers on Prayer*, translated and edited by John
Eudes Bamberger (Spencer, MA: Cistercian Publications,
1970). The *Institutes* of St. John Cassian has been newly
translated by Boniface Ramsey, O.P. (New York: Paulist,
2000). The compilation of the writings of the early monastic and ascetic writers of (mainly) the Eastern Church
known as the *Philokalia* are filled with reflections on the
eight passions; this core text of Christian spirituality is
available in English: *The Philokalia* 3 volumes (London:
Faber & Faber, 1979). John Climacus's *The Ladder of Divine Ascent*, edited by Colm Luibhead and Norman Rus-
sell (New York: Paulist, 1982) is a monastic treatise (it is
read to monks in Orthodox monasteries each Lent) that
treats the eight passions in the middle section of the treatise. There are wonderful sayings about the passions and

the deadly sins in *The Sayings of the Desert Fathers: The Alphabetical Collection*, edited by Benedicta Ward (Kalamazoo: Cistercian Publications, 1975). A briefer collection of these sayings of the desert ascetics was compiled by Thomas Merton, *The Wisdom of the Desert* (New York: New Directions, 1962), with a very useful introduction to this ancient monastic wisdom.

The classic work on the role of the seven deadly sins in the medieval West is still Morton Bloomfield's *The Seven Deadly Sins* (East Lansing: Michigan State University Press, 1952). While Bloomfield's work has a focus on English literature, the more recent study of the medievalist Aviad Kleinberg's *Seven Deadly Sins* (Cambridge, MA: Harvard University Press, 2008) is more far reaching with the added benefit of an up-to-date bibliography. The topic about the deadly sins is considered in depth in Nicholas Lombardo's *The Logic of Desire: Aquinas on Emotion* (Washington, DC: The Catholic University of America Press, 2011).

Modern writers, both religious and secular, have been interested in the seven deadly sins either because they could meditate on their modern application or simply to muse over the follies of our age. In the early days of the Second World War the English writer and Christian apologist Dorothy Sayers was invited to lecture in London to the "Public Morality Council," so she chose as her topic "The Other Six Deadly Sins," later to be published as a pamphlet under the same title (London: Methuen, 1943) for the modest price of a single shilling. Nearly forty years later the London *Times* commissioned some well-known authors to write an essay on one of the seven sins, which gave us splendid essays by notables like W. H. Auden, Evelyn Waugh, Angus Wilson, Cyril Connolly, Edith Sitwell, Christopher Sykes, and Patrick Leigh Fermor—all introduced by Ian Fleming: *The Seven Deadly Sins* (New York: Morrow, 1962).

The late Henry Fairlie found the *Times* essays "slender" and lacking in moral seriousness, so he undertook to write on the seven deadly sins for the *New Republic* in greater depth with the precise purpose of underlining something that Fairlie thought had faded in the modern consciousness: the reality of evil. Those essays are to be found in his book *The Seven Deadly Sins Today* (Notre Dame: University of Notre Dame Press, 1979). By contrast, the authors in *Wicked Pleasures: Meditations on the Seven "Deadly" Sins*, edited by Robert Solomon (Lanham: Rowan & Littlefield, 1999), write with something between "amusement" and "skepticism," as the editor describes these meditations. Despite this somewhat haughty attitude, the contributions are not without insight. By contrast, Gabriele Taylor's *Deadly Vices* (Oxford: Clarendon, 2006) is a tightly argued, immensely learned, and demanding work by a professional philosopher, who begins her book by asserting that these sins are correctly named "deadly" and correctly numbered.

Rebecca K. DeYoung's *Glittering Vices* (Grand Rapids: Brazos, 2009) is both a study of the seven deadly sins and their remedies, written from a Christian perspective. Her notes mention a number of works on the sins written from an Evangelical perspective, but, alas, the book lacks a bibliography. The Methodist preacher and theologian has published a series of homilies on the sins under the title *Sin Like a Christian* (Nashville: Abingdon, 2005). Both books take into account the contemporary situation. Finally, in 2003 the New York Public Library held a series of lectures on the seven deadly sins organized by the essayist Joseph Epstein. The following year the lectures were published as very short books by Oxford University Press; the volumes were: *Envy* by Joseph Epstein, *Greed* by Phyllis Tickle, *Gluttony* by Francine Prose, *Pride* by Michael Eric Dyson, *Anger* by Robert Thurman, and *Sloth* by Wendy Wasserstein. All the volumes were, by turn, whimsical and serious, treating the sins more as vices than sins, but all were acutely aware of contemporary mores.

Lawrence S. Cunningham is the John A. O'Brien Emeritus Professor of theology at the University of Notre Dame. A leading US scholar and award-winning professor, Cunningham is best known for his work in the areas of systematic theology and culture, Catholic spirituality, and Catholic saints.

Cunningham has edited or written over twenty-five books and is the Christianity editor of the forthcoming *Norton Anthology of World Religions*. His most recent books are *Things Seen and Unseen* and *An Introduction to Catholicism*. Cunningham has won three Catholic Press Association awards for religious writing and has been the "Booknotes" columnist for *Commonweal* for over ten years.

Founded in 1865, Ave Maria Press,
a ministry of the Congregation of
Holy Cross, is a Catholic publishing
company that serves the spiritual and
formative needs of the Church and its
schools, institutions, and ministers;
Christian individuals and families; and
others seeking spiritual nourishment.

For a complete listing of titles from

Ave Maria Press

Sorin Books

Forest of Peace

Christian Classics

visit www.avemariapress.com

ave maria press® / Notre Dame, IN 46556
A Ministry of the United States Province of Holy Cross